D0733170

Kitchen
Appliances
101:

What Works,
What Doesn't and Why

Donald E. Silvers, CKD
Moorea Hoffman

NMI Publishers
Tarzana, California

Revised Edition
Published by
NMI Publishers
18345 Ventura Boulevard,
Suite 314
Tarzana, CA 91356

Library of Congress Catalog Number:
ISNB: 0932767-10-9
Printed in the United States of America

ACKNOWLEDGEMENTS

We would like to thank the following people for their valuable input on our manuscript. Their insights helped us polish our text and refine our technical information and descriptions.

Robert Christensen, of Baker and Wells

Will Farasat, of Bay Cities Appliances

Dyanne Hoffman

Maureen Lucas

Mary Murphy

Sally Silvers

Mike Goldberg

Ted Stout

Chris Vaughan

Cover Design by Helena Rogers

Special thanks to Michael Davis of Capital Distributing for not only reading the text and giving us insightful comments, but also for suggesting we write this book.

Special thanks to Laurie Merrill and 20/20 Software, version 6.1, for providing many of the illustrations for this book.

Special thanks to Jerry Newmark for being my mentor all these years and going through the book page by page with us.

Special thanks to Sally Silvers for her time-consuming, word-by-word, editing, proof-reading, and life-saving efforts.

CONTENTS

WEIGHTS AND MEASURES.

For most preparations, it is easier to measure than to weigh.

25. *Solids.*

Butter, when soft,	one pound . . .	is one quart.
Eggs, ...	ten	are one pound.
Flour, Wheat, . .	one pound . . .	is one quart.
Meal, Indian, . .	one pound two ounces	is one quart.
Sugar, best Brown,	one pound two ounces	is one quart.
Sugar, Loaf, broken,	one pound . . .	is one quart.
Sugar, White, powdered, }	one pound one ounce	is one quart.
Flour, ...	four quarts . . .	are half a peck.
Flour, ...	sixteen quarts . .	are half a bushel.

26. *Liquids.*

Four Spoonfuls are	half a gill.
Eight Spoonfuls are	one gill.
Two Gills, or sixteen Spoonfuls are .	half a pint.
Two Pints are	one quart.
Four Quarts are	one gallon.
Twenty-five Drops are	one teaspoonful.
Four Spoonfuls are	one wineglassful.
Twelve Spoonfuls are	one teacupful.
Sixteen Spoonfuls, or half a Pint, are .	one tumblerful.

Whenever the word *spoonful* or *spoonfuls*, is used, in this work, a large, or *table-spoon*, is meant. But as measures of the same name differ in capacity, it will require judgment and practice to be familiar with due proportions.

Introduction

"Kitchens are the heart of the home." This phrase has become widespread—from HGTV to your local appliance center, you will hear it repeated like a mantra. What is not so well understood is that appliances are the heart of the kitchen. Like the heart to the body, appliances are the engine that drives what a kitchen does: cooking, cleaning, and preserving with a lot of living mixed in. With this critical importance comes an awesome responsibility to make the right choices for your family, your home, and your life. Luckily for today's consumer, the appliance industry has evolved to bring you a dazzling array of options and the opportunity to fulfill your needs and dreams. Whether you are a consumer, a designer, an architect or a builder, you face the problem of deciding not just what appliances to buy but whom to trust when looking for information. This book is your guide into this world—a guide to understanding your needs and understanding the many appliances that can satisfy them.

In our previous book, <u>Kitchen Design with Cooking in Mind</u>, our goal was to make kitchens both functional and beautiful. In this book, we focus on appliances because they are the key to a successful kitchen remodel or custom home construction. Too many times we have seen beautiful kitchens that were a disaster because the wrong appliances were chosen. Consumers are at the mercy of their designer or appliance salesperson, who in all the years of his education was never asked to boil water, let alone put on a meal for

tip It is not enough to have a pretty kitchen. It should also be a workshop and with the right appliances, you can have both.

eight or more people. It is our contention that when the months of design and construction are over and thousands of dollars have been spent, it is not enough to have a pretty kitchen. It should also be a workshop—and with the right appliances, you can have both.

We lecture extensively on kitchen design. Invariably, two thirds of the questions are about kitchen appliances—what kind they need, where to put them, how to maintain them. The people who come to see us are desperate for answers because what they've encountered is misinformation, wrong information and bad information. They hungrily ask question after question because the facts they require are not available to the public. No appliance company wants to put its product side by side with another in an objective study. If you visit three appliance stores and ask for the best oven, you will probably get three different answers. This book is for every person who left one of our seminars saying to themselves, "I never would have known; I almost made a huge mistake," and for every person who has left an appliance store more confused than when they entered, or didn't even know enough to be confused. In fact, this book is for every person buying kitchen appliances, whether it's in the context of a complete kitchen remodel or replacement in an existing space.

In the commercial kitchen design world, a kitchen designer and the restaurant owner can visit the gas or electric company's food service facilities and test, side by side, five or six different brands of ranges, steamers, ovens, tilt pans or any other piece of commercial cooking equipment. Unfortunately for consumers, there is nowhere for them to get a side-by-side working comparison of a kitchen appliance. Therefore, the choice boils down to "what color do you want" because factual information about how it works isn't available—at least not from someone who has objectively tested it rather than someone who makes his living selling it. To complicate matters, leading consumer magazines, which pretend objective study, often use criteria that is irrelevant in terms of the cooking process. Although these magazines may have good information on repair records, don't rely on them to understand how an appliance actually cooks, stores, cools or cleans. To get the answers that give you the information you need, you have to start by asking the right questions.

One way of getting this information is by going to distributor showrooms that have working appliances. However, these facilities don't offer a side-by-side comparison of different manufacturers, so you may have to go to two or three different distributors to see the models you want. Bring with you your biggest pot and the ingredients to cook your favorite dish that you make frequently, and you will really begin to see the differences from

tip No matter how much you enjoy cooking, one hour's worth of work should take you one hour–not two or more–but the wrong appliances will do just that. The choice you make in your appliances today can limit or expand your menu choices for the life of your kitchen.

model to model. That brings me to an important point about this book. We don't mention specific models or brand names because our purpose is to give you the information to analyze the quality and utility of products on your own. Products change from year to year and the manufacturer of the finest cooktop this year may make the worst next year. Be sure to ask your salesperson about warranties and make sure you read what the company is offering.

Recently, we were asked to create a curriculum about

kitchen appliances. The company wanted the course to be accredited by IDCEC (the Interior Design Continuing Education Council). That organization does the work for the American Society of Interior Designers (ASID), the Interior Designers of Canada (IDC), the Interior Design Educators Council (IDEC), the International Interior Design Association (IIDA) and the National Kitchen and Bath Association (NKBA). Their list of subjects included ten major categories and over 70 subcategories. Nowhere was the topic "kitchen appliances" mentioned. To us that is devastating as it reflects how many interior and kitchen designers and builders are not taught the skills required to evaluate the consumer's kitchen using the different kitchen appliances on the marketplace.

These designers and other kitchen industry professionals excuse their ignorance about appliances and the cooking process with the often-repeated line, "It doesn't matter, Don. They don't cook anyway." Well, this is just not true. In 2002, a consumer attitudes study published in Time magazine found that 85% of Americans say they eat home-cooked meals three or four times a week. This figure is up 11% from the year **tip** Well chosen kitchen appliances allow you to compress or expand the space in your kitchen to accommodate a simple meal for one or a complex meal for twenty. before which indicates a trend towards home-cooked meals, rather than away. Add to that the robust sales of the cookbook and cooking class industries—and the enormous popularity of the Food Channel—and the message is clear that Americans want to cook—if only their kitchens would let them.

Although there are many approaches to kitchen design,

e.g., the kitchen triangle, nowhere does residential kitchen design literature talk about volume. Simply put, "How many people can you seat in your dining room?" Once you answer that question, it speaks loudly to the kind of kitchen equipment you need. A kitchen remodel with a dining room seating four will be treated differently than one with a dining room seating twelve in determining what kind of cooktop you buy, what size refrigerator, or whether you'll need one or two ovens. Another factor overlooked is time-savings. While cooking is an important recreational activity for many of our clients, it is also a necessary activity and no matter how much you enjoy cooking, one hour's worth of work should take you one hour—not two or more—but the wrong appliances will make you do just that.

The choice you make in your appliances today can limit or expand your menu choices for the life of your kitchen. Most of us deliberately simplify our menus because our kitchens don't allow us many options. Many people think the ability to sauté, steam, and grill at the same time is impossible—so typically they limit themselves to the most ubiquitous of menus—e.g. a salad made in the sink, a roast with baked potatoes in the oven, a vegetable cooked on top of the stove and a dessert either bought or made in advance. Anything more interesting demands so much extra labor due to the inadequacies of our kitchen appliances that we usually don't attempt it. If we do, we start cooking Saturday's dinner on Wednesday. The true joy of making such a meal is thus diminished or missing altogether.

Well chosen kitchen appliances allow you to compress or expand the space in your kitchen to accommodate a simple meal for one or a complex meal for twenty. We can take a ten by ten foot space, put in the appropriate appliances in direct relationship to the volume of the dining room, and make it work wonderfully. On the other hand, we can take a fifteen by twenty foot kitchen, put in the wrong appliances in regards to volume, and render the kitchen useless.

Appliances are the key to a successful kitchen remodel or custom home construction. They determine the menus you can cook for the life of the kitchen. Too often, choice boils down to looks because factual information is hard to find. After the months of design and construction are over and thousands of dollars have been spent, it is not enough to have a pretty kitchen. It should also be a workshop—and with the right appliances, you can have both.

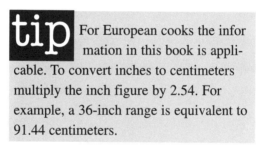

tip For European cooks the information in this book is applicable. To convert inches to centimeters multiply the inch figure by 2.54. For example, a 36-inch range is equivalent to 91.44 centimeters.

NOTES

Cooktops

How To Determine Your Needs

The most important, most frequently used and most flexible appliance in today's kitchen is your stovetop. It may come in the form of a cooktop, with separate ovens, or as a range, having burners and ovens in one unit. In either case, today's cook faces an overwhelming litany of choices. How do you determine your needs and evaluate what's on the market with your kitchen in mind? Your kitchen is only part of what will determine your cooktop needs. Just as important, but often ignored, is the size of your dining room. Cooktop choices boil down to volume, and the number of seats in your dining room is what tells you the maximum volume for which your kitchen should be designed.

What A Good Cooktop Will Do That The Average One Can't

The best example we can give that demonstrates how your choice of cooktop and other appliances affect your life is by way of a recipe. You've decided to host a dinner party for eight. The entrée you've chosen to prepare is mango chutney chicken. The recipe reads as follows:

8 chicken breasts (skinned and trimmed)

Flour for dredging chicken

1/2 cup dry white wine

2 oz. orange liqueur

16 oz. of mango chutney

(since chutney consistencies vary, you want to have extra on hand)

Wine or chicken stock (approx. 2 to 3 cups)

Pepper to taste

Preheat the oven to 425 degrees. Cover the bottom of a 13 inch frying pan with a thin layer of olive oil and heat over high flame until the oil is very hot. Dredge the breasts in flour, place in pan and fry over the high flame until browned on one side. Turn the breasts over and lower the heat. Add the wine and simmer until the liquid is reduced by half. Add the liqueur and ignite, agitating the pan as the alcohol burns off. Again reduce the liquid by half. Continue simmering the breasts until they are two-thirds cooked.

Remove the breasts from the frying pan and place on an oven rack set in a broiler pan. Pour mango chutney into the frying pan and heat over a low flame, adding wine or chicken stock as needed to achieve a medium consistency. (Keep in mind that the flour residue will thicken the sauce: it should be just thick enough to stay on the breast). When the sauce is heated thoroughly, ladle a small amount over each breast, keeping the remainder warm to spoon over the chicken before serving. Pour either the remaining wine or chicken stock (or water, in a pinch) into the bottom of the broiler pan to prevent the breasts from drying out. Reduce oven heat to 375 degrees (oven heat diminishes about one degree per second when the door is open, which is why you always want to preheat your oven about 50 degrees higher than the recommended cooking temperature. Once the food is in the oven, lower the heat to the appropriate baking temperature). Bake breasts for 15 minutes. Place on a warm platter. Spoon the remaining sauce over the top and serve.

Now that you've read the recipe, you realize you can't make the dish in your kitchen exactly the way it was written. If you have an average stove, your burners are simply too small and weak to properly heat a 13-inch frying pan. You might consider using three separate pans to accommodate all the breasts, but give it up because the burners are too close together and you don't have enough heat. You might consider frying the breasts in three separate batches, but that is too much work and the breasts might dry out. The only other way is to use the oven. Now the process has to change. The chicken breasts must be raw when placed on the oven rack. You must spoon the sauce over them, but the sauce, too, is altered. There are no pan drippings in it now so it has lost a good bit of flavor, and it is thinner since there is no flour to thicken it. You need to bake the breasts for 25 to 30 minutes. Sounds simple, easier? You're right but the chicken doesn't taste as good. Pan-frying gives the flour-dredged chicken a crunchy surface, while keeping the breasts tender and soft on the inside. The textured surface also helps hold the sauce in place. In addition, the chicken breasts have a far more beautiful color when pan-fried, thanks to the liqueur's glazing effect.

For anyone who cares about cooking and about eating well, the differences in appearance, taste, texture and smell are painfully apparent. I don't mean to suggest this is the only way to cook. I do believe, however, that you should have the option. Your kitchen should be filled with options and, most important, should respond to your specific needs.

In our previous book, <u>Kitchen Design with Cooking in Mind</u>, we discussed how inadequate counter space forces a cook to work vertically rather than horizontally. A poorly designed cooktop will victimize you in the same way. If your burners are small and close together, you must use smaller, taller pots, which require you to constantly stir the contents so the food at the bottom doesn't burn and the food at the top isn't undercooked. Think about it: How many recipes have you read requiring top of the stove cooking that you realized you couldn't prepare because your burners were inadequate?

Generally speaking, the four factors to consider when buying a cooktop are the number of burners, the distance between the burners, the adequacy and range of heat from high (sauté) to low (simmer), and the ease of maintenance. Having said that, we must add that almost none of the low to mid-price American or European cooktops work particularly well. Most are poorly designed. The burners are not large enough, they do not emit enough heat and they are badly placed in relationship to one another. (See Illustration, Figures A-G, Page 28,).

Cooktop manufacturers have not kept pace with today's cooks. Take sautéing, which requires large front burners that give off high heat. You would think manufacturers would place high heat burners up front where they belong. Unfortunately, that's not the case. Most cooktops have one small and one large burner in front; others have two small burners in front and the larger burners in back. Those configurations made some sense at one time, when a small front burner was needed to melt butter or do other tasks requiring a small pan and a low flame. But today, microwave ovens take care of those kinds of jobs faster and better. What we now need from our cooktops are larger burners with better control—burners that can handle a 13-inch pan when cooking for large groups and that can quickly switch from high heat for sautéing to low heat for poaching or simmering.

Have you ever asked a restaurant chef to give you the

recipe for a certain dish you love, tried it at home, and it just did-n't work? He insists he gave you the right recipe; you insist he must have left out a secret ingredient. What the two of you do not realize is that the key ingredient is heat. The intensity and consis-tency of heat is going to affect the taste and texture of your food.

One of the most important considerations for any cook purchasing a cooktop is the strange term "recovery ratio." Recovery ratio, a crucial consideration in the commercial kitchen world, is no less important for the home cook. This term describes the amount of time it takes for the fat or liquid in the pan to get back to the temperature it had reached before the food to be cooked was added. Think of making pasta. You bring the water to a rapid boil, then add a dash of salt to make the water roll faster. You add the pasta and the water immediately stops boiling. The recovery ratio is the amount of time it takes for the water to again come to a boil. The lag time matters less for boiling pasta than it does for, say, pan-frying, when you start by heating some type of oil or butter and then add the poultry, fish or meat. Immediately, the oil or fat loses much of its heat. *The slower the recovery ratio of your cooktop, the greasier your food will turn out.* Not to men-tion less juicy and flavorful.

Recovery ratio is controlled by the heat output of the burn-er—the higher the heat, the faster the recovery ratio. On gas burners, heat is measured in British Thermal Units (BTUs). One BTU equals the amount of heat required to raise the temperature of one pound of water one degree. In an electrically powered cooktop, energy is measured in watts. Watts translate to BTUs on the order of roughly one to four: 1,000 watts equals about 4,000 BTUs. An electric cooktop's large burner, or element, generates

1,000 to 2,700 watts, which equals 4,000 to 10,800 BTUs, while the small elements run 600 to 1,000, or 2,400 to 4,000 BTUs, technically. I say "technically" because gas cooktops lose 25 to 35 percent of their heat (unless the burner is sealed) so an electric cooktop's large element is roughly equivalent to something more like a 14,000 BTU gas burner.

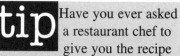

Have you ever asked a restaurant chef to give you the recipe for a certain dish you love, tried it at home, and it just didn't work? He insists he gave you the right recipe; you insist he must have left out a secret ingredient. What the two of you do not realize is that the key ingredient is heat.

Fuel Source Options

We are often asked what type of cooktop we recommend. You have basically three choices: gas, electric, or magnetic induction. Gas is the most popular by far, so let's start there.

• **Gas**. Professional cooks use gas more than any other source of heat. Of course, they're playing in the big leagues. A burner on a professional cooktop generates between 25,000 and 35,000 BTUs. The vast majority of cooktops or stoves sold to consumers range in BTUs between 6,000 and 9,000. If you are lucky, you may have one burner that goes as high as 12,000 BTUs. This disparity in available heat can make a significant difference in the quality of the food you're sautéing.

Gas provides the home cook with the greatest number of options. You can see the size of your flame, and you can control it instantly, bringing the heat up or down. Gas cooktops feature combinations of one, two, four, five, six or eight burners and run from 12" wide for single burner units to 60" wide for the ten burner models. They are anywhere from 19- to 27-inches deep. As I've mentioned, you want to know the amount of BTUs the burners generate, the size of the grate that the pot or pan sits on, and the distance between the burners. You also want to know how large a pan will fit on each burner. Shopping for a cooktop becomes much easier if you take along your largest frying pan or stockpot.

There are two styles of gas cooktops on the marketplace today—the drop-in cooktop and the range top, sometimes inappropriately called a professional style cooktop, but we'll get to that later. Standard drop-in cooktops are 30- to 45-inches wide and 19- to 21-inches deep. They are designed to fit into a hole cut into the countertop with a height of at most 5-inches, allowing almost all of the cabinet under them to be used as storage. These models usually have four to six burners. There are a few companies that make 12- or 15-inch one burner cooktops—some with high BTU burners that nicely complement other cooking surfaces in large kitchens. These units can be part of a modular system or they can be used individually.

By far, the most popular version of the drop-in cooktop is 36-inches wide with five burners. The best models put the knobs to one side, rather than in the center, so you have room to slide pots around and can use 13-inch pans without being concerned that the pan will prevent you from reaching the knobs (See Illustration, Figure F-G, Page 28). Most of these units have one high heat burner (usually between 12,000 and 15,000 BTUs) in the center with one small and one medium output burner in front and the same in back. The best units have burners that are all the same size, with the ability to set the flame to a simmer or sauté temperature on every one. The main drawback to this kind of unit is its narrow depth. Twenty-one inches is small enough so that one large pot per side is about all you can manage, making the 30-inch wide models almost impossible to work with.

Another disadvantage to the 30-inch drop-in cooktop is the knob location. We have already mentioned that the knobs work better to the side than in the center, but even the side position is inferior to the front face-mount position of knobs on range-tops. Top-mounted knobs are difficult to read from anywhere but right next to the cooktop, and for safety's sake you should be able to glance at the cooktop from across the room and see the setting, or at least whether or not a burner is on.

tip You may be wondering about this 13-inch pan we keep mentioning—is it really necessary? Yes! This size pan allows you to pan-fry or sauté for six to nine people in one pan which means less work, fewer pots to clean and many more menu choices.

Some people are concerned that knobs on the front of a machine will be tempting to small children. However, the dexterity and hand strength required to push in and turn these knobs is probably more than a young child would be able to accomplish.

You may be wondering about this 13-inch pan we keep mentioning—is it really necessary? Yes! This size pan allows you to pan-fry or sauté for six to nine people in one pan which means less work, fewer pots to clean and many more menu choices.

Rangetops are sometimes misnamed "professional" or "pro-style" cooktops. These models have, nothing to do with the ranges used by restaurant chefs. For example, they have around 16,000 BTUs while truly commercial cooktop burners have 25,000 to 35,000 BTUs. Many consumers are intimidated by these appliances because of that terrible name. In reality, range-tops should be called multi-purpose cooktops. Although they have the reputation of being a high-end extravagance, the truth is they benefit every cook, whether he or she considers her cooking "gourmet" or simply utilitarian. These cooktops will help your

tip Many consumers are intimidated by so-called "professional" cooktops because of that terrible name. In reality, range-tops should be called multi-purpose cooktops. Although they have the reputation of being a high-end extravagance, the truth is they benefit every cook, whether he or she considers her cooking "gourmet" or simply utilitarian.

skills in the kitchen grow, taking your cooking to the next level. The difference between these units and the cooktop the average consumer struggles with is the ease and volume of quality food they enable you to produce at one time. You can sauté your vegetables, simmer your sauce, and boil your pasta simultaneously. They are the natural evolution of cooktops from previous generations.

The dimensions of rangetops are both higher and deeper than cooktops. They are designed to fit on top of a cabinet between two sections of counter (See Illustration, Figures L-M, Page 28). They are 24- to 27-inches deep front to back and have the knobs on the front of the unit, rather than on the cooking surface. That maximizes the amount of room you have up top for pots and pans and will allow two large pans to fit front to back, unlike a drop-in cooktop. They typically have between 15,000 and 18,000 BTUs per burner and usually all the burners have the same range from high to low heat, allowing the cook greater flexibility and ease. Have you ever been cooking something on a burner only to realize the amount of heat needed meant moving the pot to a different burner? That problem plagues the owners of ninety percent of the cooktops produced today—the combination of large and small burners create work and force you to cook a certain way in a certain place. Many clients assume they don't need a multi-purpose cooktop that big, that powerful and that looks so commercial. But looks can be deceiving. Those are the only cooktops that give you all your options.

Sometimes, well-meaning advisors—whether friends, salespeople or even designers—will say, "You don't really need so much power in your cooktop." The two most common statements are, "Don't worry about it, they don't cook anyway," or "Why waste your money keeping up with the Joneses?" They are thinking about the minimum requirements—what you need to make a quick meal for your family. It is certainly possible to make a meal on the average cooktop, but it will be an average meal.

Appliances should always be chosen with the maximum, not the minimum, requirements in mind. If Thanksgiving is an important holiday in your family, you wouldn't buy an oven that **tip** Appliances should always be chosen with the maximum, requirements in mind, never the minimum. couldn't fit a good-sized turkey—and Thanksgiving only comes once a year. How many potentially terrific meals would be missed—even on weekdays—because you made your cooktop selection based on what you usually do, rather than what you could do? Ask yourself, "What is the maximum number of guests I would like to cook for, how many and what kinds of dishes would I like to make?" Great pleasure, excitement, and relaxation are possible when cooking is fun and meals are varied and creative. Don't trap yourself "inside the box" of the 30-inch standard cooktop or range.

Lets talk about the components that make up a good cooktop. In addition to providing the cook with high and low BTUs on each and every burner, good cooktops are made of quality materials that will hold up to high heat over time. Look for models with brass valves, not aluminum. The burner caps should feel heavy and solid in your hand. The grates should be solid, but not so heavy that you have trouble lifting them out of the way to clean underneath.

Easy clean-up is an important feature of any kitchen appliance. Cooktops with sealed burners far outshine **tip** As with most good things, the sealed burner cooktop is more expensive to manufacture and therefore more expensive to buy, but the drudgery you avoid is well worth the investment. their open burner counterparts in that department. In an open-burner model, there is an opening between the gas burner and the surrounding cooktop surface, which may be stainless steel or enamel coated porcelain. Particles of food, oil or water that spill will drip through the opening onto a catch-pan. Most gas cooktops are made that way. In the better open-burner models, the catch pan is a tray that slides out of the front of the machine and can be wiped clean. Lower end models require you to remove the cooktop surface and reach inside to clean. As the name implies, sealed burners do not have the opening, so you have one surface to clean (the top of the cooktop) instead of two (top and catch pan). As with most good things, the sealed burner cooktop is more expensive to manufacture and therefore more expensive to buy, but the drudgery you avoid is well worth the investment.

We have a couple of cautions about cooktops with sealed and heavy-duty burners that generate 12,000 BTUs and up. With some of those cooktops, simmering can be difficult without the use of a heat diffuser, or metal plate, that sits between the pan and the burner grate to lower the amount of heat transferred. Luckily, heat diffusers are inexpensive and can be found at most hardware or kitchen supply stores. Be sure to check with the cooktop manufacturer to see if you can simmer on every burner without the use of a heat diffuser. Some cooktops only have one dedicated simmer burner instead of all burners having equal simmer capability but, again, that limits your choices.

Also be wary of any continuous grate, often times referred to as an "S" or "V" grate because of the design (See Illustration, Figure O, Page 28). Even when you turn the heat down, the temperature will remain constant for a considerable length of time. If you want to simmer, you will have to slide the pot or pan to another area of the cooktop. That type of grate can also be difficult to wash because of its additional weight.

• **Electric**. Most electric cooktops, which generate about the same energy as gas cooktops, have all the same inherent problems—not enough heat, small element size, and not enough distance between elements. Still, some clients prefer them. They claim electric is cleaner and produces no gas fumes, which is certainly true.

tip Our advice for electric cooktop users who know they will need both high and low heat while cooking is to pre-heat two elements, one high and one low. Then simply move your pan to the appropriate burner when you need to rapidly increase or decrease temperature.

Most electric cooktops come with

two, four, five, or six elements. We recommend six, since the response time for heating and cooling elements is laboriously slow. In fact, the wait can drive you crazy. Our advice for electric cooktop users who know they will need both high and low heat while cooking is to pre-heat two elements, one high and one low. Then simply move your pan to the appropriate burner when you need to rapidly increase or decrease temperature.

Electric cooktops offer a choice of element styles—coil or ceramic glass top. Coil, a metal heating element in a spiral shape, allows you to see if the heat is on or off, since the coil turns red when hot. What some people like is the constant heat with little variation once it's set. Ceramic glass tops can be damaged by heat that's too intense, and because large pots and pans tend to trap the heat, they can cause the element to turn off. The electric elements have a built-in temperature swing because the temperature is controlled by a thermostat designed to protect the glass—turning on and off rather than maintaining a constant temperature. That poses a lot of problems for any activity that requires steady heat or requires heat to build up over time. Some people claim ceramic glass tops are easiest to wipe clean. However, you can't see the heat and certain spills can create a real cleaning problem because they may burn onto the cooktop, becoming almost impossible to remove.

• **Magnetic Induction** . The only type of pots or pans you can use on a magnetic induction cooktop are those made of ferrous metal—test any pan with a simple fridge magnet; if it sticks you can use it. Unlike traditional cooktops, magnetic induction surfaces do not have a direct heat source, such as a flame or coil.

Magnetic induction works by causing the pan's metal molecules to vibrate, thus creating energy, which generates heat. The cooktop itself stays cool, although, after the pan is removed, you can feel the heat left by the pan's bottom.

Magnetic induction, while absolutely superb for low heat tasks—such as melting chocolate or butter, steaming and poaching—has in the past been unable to generate enough heat to adequately sauté. Given sufficient time, a cast-iron skillet will be able to reach a sufficient temperature, but it will also stay hot for a long time since cast iron dissipates heat relatively slowly. Thus, you lose control over the cooking process.

However, there are some new products on the market that claim to have 3,000 watts, enough to generate the kind of heat necessary to achieve a decent recovery ratio. One company is producing an induction wok unit which promises the equivalent of 35,000 BTUs! Test those units before you buy because not all induction burners are created equal. For the high-rise dweller currently locked into an electric cooktop, induction models are a godsend. They allow instant temperature control without pesky heat fluctuations and have far less ventilation requirements than traditional gas or electric models.

For units with lower wattage, you can achieve a flexible, efficient cooking surface by adding two high BTU gas burners to your kitchen set-up. If space allows, place them side by side with 13,000 or more BTU capacity. This combination of gas and magnetic induction gives you the best of both worlds—options that give you high heat and efficient low heat that is easily accessible. In addition, if the power ever goes out, you will still be able to put a meal together.

Other Cooking Surfaces and Equipment

There are a few other choices and necessities you need to consider before your cooking decisions are complete:

• **Charbroilers**. With today's emphasis on low-fat cooking, charbroilers (sometimes called grills) are a terrific addition to any kitchen. Those units usually consist of an iron grill over a gas or electric burner, with simulated charcoal briquettes or stainless steel diffusers in between and a catch pan underneath. Not only are meat and fish wonderfully tasty, but vegetables are extraordinary.

Although you can choose between gas and electric charbroilers, the smart choice is gas because it offers almost an additional thousand degrees of heat (Harold McGee <u>On Food and Cooking</u> p. 614). The flavor in grilling comes from melting fat, which hits the heat diffuser, turns to smoke, rises and adheres to the food's surface. The greater the heat, the more smoke it creates and the tastier the food. The material making up the heat diffuser also plays a critical part in whether or not the charbroiler works well. Those that have ceramic heat diffusers will have more consistent heating across the entire cooking surface so you have less difficulty with some chicken breasts cooking faster than others. They will also give you more of a grilled flavor because less of the oil will drip to the catch pan. Stainless steel diffusers, although easy to maintain, don't do a good job of catching that liquid and heating it up. They also increase flare-ups. Ceramic diffusers come in many shapes—briquettes, rods, dominoes and so on. We have not noticed that the shape of the ceramic diffuser much affects its performance.

In today's market, gas charbroilers are available as an integral part of your rangetop or range (See Illustration, Figure K, Page 28). They are typically combined with four burners in a 36-inch rangetop or range, or with six burners in a 48-inch range-top or range. With these models, the grill takes the place of two burners. There are also 24- and 30-inch wide charbroilers that are separate units. Be aware that any charbroiler added to your cook-ing surface will require additional ventilation from your hood—see the ventilation chapter for details. Also, you should not put a shelf over the grill because the shelf will be very difficult to keep clean and could reduce the efficiency of your ventilation. Look for a grill with a stainless steel cover, so that your charbroiler could be used as additional counter space when not in use. Also ensure the model you select has a removable catchpan to collect drippings.

For years, Don had a love/hate relationship with his gas charbroiler. He loved cooking on it but hated cleaning it. He was tempted to throw it in his self-cleaning oven, but the manufactur-er's instructions said not to, lest the porcelain finish burn off the grate. Porcelain, aside from its general attractiveness, helps to prevent foods from sticking. Then one day a client of his said damaging the porcelain finish doesn't matter. The client told Don to brush the charbroiler with an oil that had a high burning point (such as corn oil) before using it and the food would never stick. Then the grate can be placed in a self-cleaning oven. Suddenly clean-up became a breeze.

Here is a tip to help you maintain your grill—when your grill is still hot from cooking, scrub the grates with a brass wire brush. For best results, you should do this each and every time you use the grill.

• **Griddles**. A griddle is essentially a built-in fry-pan. Some salespeople will confuse it with a grill (charbroiler) but don't be fooled—a griddle works very differently. At first glance, griddles seem like a good idea. The positive feature is the ease with which you can cook pancakes, crepes, bacon, sausages, tortillas and any other food you would normally cook in a frying pan with low sides. However, you lose two burners in order to accommodate a griddle. Griddles also do not allow an immediate adjustment of heat. They are high maintenance, requiring frequent oiling to prevent rust, and may be dangerous when there are children around since there is no visible heat source. For most consumers, the negatives far outweigh the positives. Instead, buy a griddle that fits on top of the range or cooktop burners, or buy an electric griddle that sits on the counter.

• **Wok Burners**. Stir-frying demands extremely high heat. Generally, the BTUs produced by a wok burner depend on the size of the wok you are using. In residential use, this concept is never taken into account. In the average appliance store, you will see a few gas cooktops with a large, usually centrally located burner, advertised as a "wok burner." That burner usually has between 15,000 and 18,000 BTUs. That name is about as accurate as calling a glider a jet. Real wok burners, the kind you find in the kitchen of a Chinese restaurant, can have well over 100,000 BTUs. That kind of heat is unnecessary, and even dangerous in the home environment. A few companies make a separate, single burner wok unit for residential use that has 30,000 BTUs. It is expensive, and uses up to 30 inches of counter space. But it does the job. Unless stir-fry is an important nightly meal, it will probably not be used enough to justify the expense. A high output cooktop burner will do a beautiful job of fast sautéing, which in many ways can be like stir-frying.

• **Deep-Fat Fryers and Countertop Steamers**. Deep-fat fryers need to be calibrated. The average temperature for frying is 375 degrees. Key things to look for are heavy BTUs (or watts) for recovery ratio, a way of draining the fat from the unit, and an interior made entirely of stainless steel.

Most of us think of a deep-fat fryer for frying only; however, instead of fat in the well, you can use stock and cook pasta or vegetables—so don't think of a deep-fat fryer in just the traditional sense. It can be used in a variety ways.

If you have limited cooktop space, built-in countertop steamers can help save the day. They are primarily used for steaming vegetables and poaching chicken or fish. Be sure that you can drain the unit easily and that it seals well.

Pots and Pans

Once you've selected your new cooktop, it's time to take your kitchen remodel to the next level and re-evaluate your pots and pans. When a cooktop is producing intense heat, it is important to have a pan that can distribute that heat quickly and evenly. It is equally important to have a pan that dissipates that heat quickly. The best pans have a triple-ply

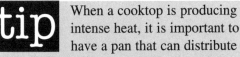

When a cooktop is producing intense heat, it is important to have a pan that can distribute that heat quickly and evenly. It is equally important to have a pan that dissipates that heat quickly.

construction, having an internal core of copper or aluminum—the best heat conducting metal commonly used in cooking equipment—and a stainless steel interior and exterior. We have found such pans to be high quality, long lasting, and easy to maintain. In some companies, the core is on the bottom of the pan only and the sides are thin stainless steel. Don't be tempted by that thick bottom—it won't do you much good. Opt for pans that have a core that extends all the way up the sides. Those pans do a much better job of transferring heat to the food without scorching the bottom layer.

A quick bit of advice about using your pots in a traditional way: Consider for a moment how you heat a can of soup. You probably put the soup into a small pot, set the flame on low, and put a cover on it. Next time you perform this task, try using a small frying pan instead. Despite the label, frying pans are an even better tool for that purpose because more of the soup comes into contact with the hot pan. This method will heat the soup faster and give you greater control and more consistent results.

Energy Efficiency

Not only do more powerful burners help you cook better, they also help you conserve energy. The more BTUs a burner produces, the faster it will cook your food. When it comes to energy efficiency, it's better to have a burner with higher heat that's on for less time rather than having low heat burn on and on. Luckily, this is usually better for the quality of your food, and a high-heat burner can always be turned down low when you need to do a long, slow simmer (osso buco, anyone?).

DROP-IN COOKTOPS

FIG. A
30" ELECTRIC COOKTOP

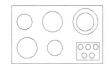

FIG. B
36" ELECTRIC COOKTOP

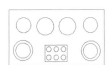

FIG. C
45" ELECTRIC COOKTOP

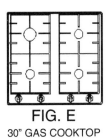

FIG. E
30" GAS COOKTOP

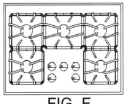

FIG. F
36" GAS COOKTOP

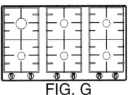

FIG. G
36" ELECTRIC COOKTOP

FIG. H
DEEP FAT FRYER

FIG. I
INDUCTION COOKTOP

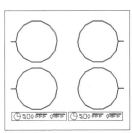

FIG. J
INDUCTION COOKTOP

All drawings copyright of 20/20 Software, version 6.1

RANGE TOPS

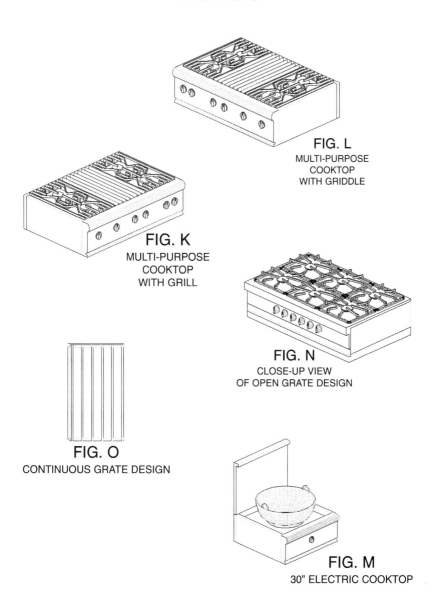

FIG. L
MULTI-PURPOSE
COOKTOP
WITH GRIDDLE

FIG. K
MULTI-PURPOSE
COOKTOP
WITH GRILL

FIG. N
CLOSE-UP VIEW
OF OPEN GRATE DESIGN

FIG. O
CONTINUOUS GRATE DESIGN

FIG. M
30" ELECTRIC COOKTOP

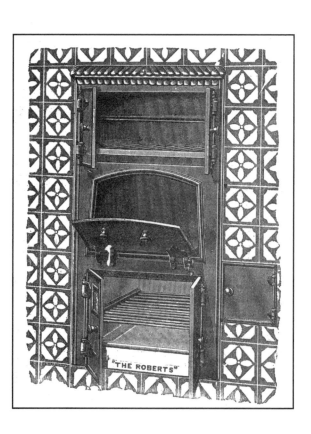

Ovens

There are a few misconceptions about ovens that we want clear up before describing how you should select yours. First, there is some confusion about what an oven does. It is impossible to roast in an oven. An oven bakes. Everywhere you look, there are cookbooks, chefs, and friends expounding the virtues of roasted red potatoes, roast chicken or other such nonsense. When you look at how these items are prepared, you see they call for an oven. This is a serious misnomer—"roasting" means cooking on a spit over an open flame. Gas barbecues can roast, ovens cannot.

In addition, there is little understanding of what an oven is. A pot on top of the stove with a lid on is an oven. A barbecue with the lid down is an oven. An oven is a closed container with a radiant or convection heat source. You can bake beautifully in your barbecue, providing it has a cover that can be closed. In the days before Moorea remodeled her kitchen, she would put a pizza stone on top of the grates in her barbecue and bake pizza, pies, and bread. It was an easy way to eke out a little extra cooking space in a cramped kitchen.

Open flames aside, there has been a virtual revolution in oven design since the days of the single range oven. No longer relegated to "wherever space can be found," today's ovens can perform an array of tasks and have become integral in good kitchen design.

Types Of Ovens And How They Work

Five types of ovens are available on the market today: the standard radiant oven, the convection oven (the true convection and the fan-assisted), the microwave oven, the convection/microwave oven and the steam oven.

• **Radiant Oven.** The radiant oven, whether heated by gas or electricity, is the one most familiar to us. Wall ovens are almost always electric. In a range, the fuel source is usually the same for the oven as it is for the burners. In higher end models, dual fuel units are available that have gas burners and an electric oven. An oven has two heating elements (burners in a gas oven)—one positioned at the top for broiling and the other at the bottom for baking. In some of the newer units, both top and bottom elements can be used for baking. In the standard radiant oven, heat rises from the bottom of the oven to the top, pushing the cold air down which can create hot and cold spots that result in uneven cooking. We all know what it's like to put two trays of cookies on an oven's two shelves. The cookies on the bottom cook much faster than those on the top because they are closer to the bottom heating element. The trays must be reversed halfway through the baking time or the cookies on the bottom will be burned, and the cookies on the top undercooked. There is a better oven on the market—the convection oven.

• **Convection Ovens.** There are actually two types of convection ovens available today: the true convection and the fan-assisted. Some domestic ovens are fan-assisted, which means that the manufacturer has added a fan to the back of the standard radiant oven. All gas ovens with fans are fan-assisted, not true convection. I'm not saying that type of oven isn't good, but it can't handle the large volume of food that a true convection oven with its additional racks and consistent heat can easily manage.

In the fan-assisted oven, the heat comes from the exposed elements at the top and bottom, with the bottom contributing 75 percent of the heat and the top contributing 25 percent. Remember, heat rises. The fan circulates the heat in the oven cavity to eliminate hot and cold spots. This type of oven generally can handle only two racks of food at a time, even though the manufacturer usually provides a third rack. If you use all three racks, you will have to rotate the food at some point, because the top and bottom racks will brown faster than the middle rack due to their direct exposure to the two heating elements.

A true convection oven differs in that a third heating element is wrapped around the fan, which causes the heat to flow evenly over all the racks. There are three or four racks in the oven, and you never need to change their positions, even for baking. But that's not the only benefit: you can simultaneously place a tray of cookies, a pan of fish, and a pan of poultry in a true convection oven. The aromas and flavors will not mingle because the direction of the airflow is from the front of the oven to the back, so that the air passes over the food, then over the heating element in the rear of the oven, and back along the sides and over the food again. During this process the particles of food that make up aroma and flavor—the oils—are burned up when the air is superheated by the element wrapped around the convection fan. The air that circulates back over the food is cleaned in that process.

Convection ovens are beginning to appeal to the consumer for the convenience that this kind of volume cooking makes possible. That brings me to an important point—the proper way to measure oven capacity: in a standard radiant oven with exposed heating elements, the cooking space is measured from the bottom rack to the top heating element. In ovens without exposed elements (the bottom element is hidden beneath the floor of the oven) the cooking space is measured from the floor of the oven to the top element. An enclosed bottom heating element is preferable because it allows you to rest a pan directly on the floor of the oven when you are cooking in convection mode. Those few inches may mean the difference between fitting three or four casseroles or four to five cookie sheets; useful, for example, when you are having a party for twelve and you have asked everyone to bring a dish. Or you could complete an entire meal in the oven. In addition, it makes clean up a breeze. One minor disadvantage to the enclosed element is that it makes the pre-heat cycle of the oven in baking mode slightly longer, as the heat must be transferred through the metal floor. Nothing should ever be set directly on the floor of the oven when it is in baking mode and the bottom element is on.

Convection ovens cook foods faster than radiant ovens. Some home cooks worry that this will make it difficult to use their favorite recipes. On the contrary, the conversion is very simple. The key is time and here is the formula: if the recipe calls for 375 degree cooking, you have two choices. The first option is to bake the item at 375 degrees in the convection oven for 25% less time than you would bake in a normal radiant oven. (For example, if the recipe calls for 375 degrees for one hour, bake the food for forty-five minutes.) Your second conversion choice is to bake the item for the same amount of time as you would in a radiant oven, but lower the heat by 25 degrees. If you are baking, choose the normal time and reduced temperature, especially with a recipe that calls for a mixture of ingredients with a leavening action, because you must allow proper time in the heat for a chemical reaction to take place. You do not want to do that quickly or the texture of your cake or cookies or bread will be compromised. Just for the fun of it, there is below a simple recipe for baked chicken or a small turkey. Keep in mind, slower cooking at lower temperatures will result in a more moist bird.

The key to this recipe is to cook the bird on a rack you create—of food! Carrots and celery work beautifully, as do onions and fennel. Using all of the above or just one of them will make a great rack. Put the layer of vegetables in the bottom of your roasting pan and put the bird on top of them, breast side down. Cook the bird at 375 degrees, approximately fifteen

tip One last note is that any recipe that calls for pre-heating at 375 degrees and baking at 375 degrees, should be pre-heated instead at 425 degrees because in the process of opening the oven door and putting the product on the rack, the oven will easily lose 50 degrees of heat.

minutes per pound (without stuffing), flipping the breast side up for the last fifteen to twenty minutes so that it will brown nicely. Because most of the fat in the bird's body is in its back, by cooking it breast side down it will baste automatically. The vegetable rack will create lots of juice, which will mingle with the fat and drippings of the chicken. Once you've pulled the bird out of the oven to let it rest, drain the fluids from the pan into a pot and thicken with a little Wondra flour (a quick-mixing flour). Be sure to cook the raw taste of the flour out of the gravy and you will have a great dish. One last note is that any recipe that calls for pre-heating at 375 degrees and baking at 375 degrees, should be pre-heated instead at 425 degrees because in the process of opening the oven door and putting the product on the rack, the oven will easily lose 50 degrees of heat.

As good as it seems, a convection oven has its problems. The forced air flow can cause dryness in some foods. Adding liquid, such as stock, wine, or water to a roasting pan helps combat the problem. But many bakers will not use convection ovens for baking items such as meringues, or anything with phyllo dough or puff pastry for just that reason.

The beauty of most convection ovens made for home use is that they can switch from convection to radiant, or radiant to convection. You have options, which, as you know by now, is our favorite word. For example, if you have a dining room that seats 10, 12, or 14 people and you are a family of 4, we suggest you consider having a smaller convection oven on top with a larger one on the bottom. Again, don't be deceived by how tiny the small, European built-in convection oven appears. It will easily handle a 20-pound turkey. So you may want two different size ovens—a small one for daily use and a larger one when entertaining crowds.

Another small addition with a lot of impact is the "convenience oven" or "half oven." These models are the same width as their big brothers but are shorter in height. Combined with full-size ovens, they reach the magic forty to forty-two inch height that allows them to easily replace many of the wall ovens sold in the seventies and eighties, without a costly cabinet retrofit. The best of these units are convection, with bake and broil features and the wonderful timers and settings of the larger ovens. They are available in 24-, 27-, and 30-inch widths. Some of these ovens have warming or toasting options, allowing you to replace a warming drawer and toaster oven with the same built-in appliance.

Convection ovens are now available in 36-inch wide models. The oven cavity in these units is 24-inches wide, which means the racks are too large to store conveniently in most standard kitchens. Be sure to have your designer specify a base cabinet that is 12- to 15-inches wide and over 24-inches high in order to store these racks vertically.

Also, keep in mind that if you use double wall ovens, or stacking ovens, you lose two to two-and-a-half feet of counterspace. If you can afford it, fine, but most small kitchens can't. Counter space comes under the heading of high frequency use, while ovens are low frequency. Placing both ovens under the counter may mean you'll have to bend a few times a week, but it may be worth the trade-off. It's your decision, but ponder it carefully. In addition, the multiple rack feature of a convection oven can double the volume of one oven, so if you are really pressed for space, a convection oven is a wise investment.

• **Microwave Ovens** . Microwaves are an energy source that cooks food from the outside in by agitating the molecules in the food, which creates friction and which in turn creates heat. They are, in essence, steam machines. In microwave ovens, the most important quality to look for is wattage; your best bet is to buy the highest possible. The reason is simple: the higher the wattage, the faster the food cooks. You want to be able to cook with low, medium, or high heat in small and distinct time units.

A good microwave oven cookbook is a must, but be aware that there is no standardization among them. Medium in one book can mean 275 degrees and in another 325 degrees, so you will need to do some experimenting with whatever microwave you choose.

Most of our clients use their microwave ovens for melting butter, warming leftovers and reheating coffee, with the occasional popcorn thrown in. For those uses, smaller units are actually more efficient than larger units because microwaves are more intense in a smaller space and the power to volume ratio is more concentrated. A few companies make models that are shallow enough to fit into a standard 12-inch deep wall cabinet (most microwave ovens are 16-inches deep and up). The shallower units actually cook better and faster than their larger counterparts and as long as they can fit your daily-use dishes they will work for whatever you need.

One innovative company has recently produced a microwave drawer. What an intelligent idea! This product has the same capacity as larger microwaves and an excellent wattage rate. Although it is more expensive than the equivalent wall- or countertop microwave, we feel the benefits equal or outway the expense. First, it is at an excellent height ergonomically. Microwaves in wall cabinets are often too high for children and even some adults to use comfortably. Many people use their microwaves to heat up soup; if the microwave is higher than your elbow height, you risk spills and burned hands. Microwaves that are combined with a rangehood are especially dangerous because they are often higher than eye level. They also create a logistical conflict. If you want to re-heat coffee while your spouse is making breakfast, the two of you will be constantly pushing each other out of the way. Not only does the microwave drawer solve these problems, it also frees up valuable counter space. It can be put into an island without forgoing function (you will sometimes see traditional microwaves used this way: it is a terrible idea because you must bend or squat to work the controls). And lastly, microwaves are not beautiful appliances. Wall cabinets are at eye level and are often the focus of the kitchen's look—a microwave discretely tucked into a drawer gives you more options for creating the scene you want.

A helpful hint about a task microwave ovens should never perform—defrosting! It is very popular today to quickly defrost items, especially meats, in the microwave. While it may be the fastest way to thaw food, it's also the fastest way to ruin a good piece of meat before you even have the chance to cook it. The fast thaw microwave defrosting produces results in a loss of the juices inside the meat. While your steak may have started out juicy, it will be dry before the cooking process begins with this defrosting method. While microwave ovens are the worst offenders, any hurried thaw will have the same effect, such as covering the meat with warm water in the sink. To avoid sabotaging

tip Never defrost food, especially meat, in a microwave oven. While it may be the fastest way to thaw food, it's also the fastest way to ruin a good piece of meat before you even have the chance to cook it.

your meal at the beginning, just think a little bit ahead of time. If you know you will be making dinner around seven, put the steaks into the refrigerator in the morning before work. That takes a little planning, but it also takes less time. The steaks will be ready to begin cooking as soon as you are, and they will have retained their fullest flavor, texture, and juiciness.

• **Combination Ovens**. Convection/microwave ovens are hybrid creatures that have come into their own in the last few years. I am not referring here to any type of portable countertop unit. I am talking about a full size, built-in oven, which runs roughly from 24- to 30-inches wide, 12- to 18-inches high and 18- to 24-inches deep. These ovens have the capacity to cook by microwave or convection heat or both. The best, most versatile of the breed require the same 220 volt electrical connection as an electric oven, rather than the standard 110 volt used by microwaves.

Combination ovens can be of great help to the working person who likes to have a home-cooked meal but does not have a lot of time in which to cook it. These ovens allow you, in most cases, to throw in a little microwave power while cooking with convection methods. These models won't change the texture of the food being cooked as much as a standard microwave oven. However, like most appliances that try to combine two separate functions into the same machine, you often end up with an appliance that can perform two tasks with mediocrity rather than one task well. While a convection/microwave will microwave anything you put into it, don't expect it to replace your small countertop unit that efficiently concentrates the energy in its small cavity. Food takes longer to microwave in a combination oven because the microwave energy diminishes within the larger cavity. You might say that it gets "lost in space."

Combination cooking works well with almost any baked good. An apple pie can be baked in half the time and still produce a brown, flaky crust. Many casseroles also do well, but meats do not since microwaving rubberizes meat.

• **Steam Ovens**. Technically, that title is a misnomer. Steam ovens are really steam machines, not ovens. There are a few models available to the consumer and although they may seem like a specialized appliance, they are in reality applicable to many different foods and many different ways of cooking. Steam cooking creates a moist, flavorful result that leaves nutrients intact and does not require a lot of oils or sauces. Its health benefits are undeniable, but these machines create a very different result than stovetop steamers.

The first unit we will discuss is pure steamer—it does not function as an oven at all. This unit does not need specialized plumbing—the cook fills the water reservoir from the sink tap. The water is superheated into steam in a special chamber, and then the steam is released into the cooking cavity. Because of the intense heat and the rapid release of steam, the color, texture, and taste of food is well preserved. That is very different from what happens when you steam on the stove, where the heat builds up slowly over time. This drawn-out process of steaming often results in limp foods because the more time the food spends in the heat, the more the vitamins and proteins will break down, resulting in bland color and limp texture.

Rapid, intense cooking is the best way to cook vegetables to seal in their flavor and retain the vitamins and minerals they naturally contain. Steamers are also superior to microwaves in their ability to reheat many foods without affecting texture. They are also more convenient. Steaming in your microwave usually requires that you set the machine, cook, stop, and stir, reset and go again. A steamer will cook vegetables as quickly as a microwave but with much better results. They work especially well for large volume cooking. For Example, in a microwave each potato requires an additional increment of time, where a steamer will do any volume of potatoes in the same amount time. In a microwave, you can steam a potato in 3 minutes, but two potatoes requires six minutes, three potatoes nine minutes and so on. A steam machine will steam any number of potatoes in just three minutes.

Steam machines also work well for poaching chicken and fish. When used in tandem with an oven, they can also be used for cooking fatty meats like ribs. Steam the meat until partially cooked and then brown and finish in an oven.

There is another steam oven available that is both steam machine and convection oven. This type of appliance has been in the commercial market for many years under the name combo oven. Finally, it has come to the residential market. And what a marvelous instrument it is. It allows you either steam or bake, or do both simultaneously. It even lets you change the humidity of the

tip For that small kitchen where you have minimal room, one convection oven plus the Combo can replace a double oven and microwave.

interior cavity, which gives you an array of options for the cooking of fish, fowl, and meat. In addition, you have the ability to cook in volume.

Generally, when we think of steaming, we think of poaching. And we all know that steaming doesn't do a great job with meat, other than poached. But in the combo oven, because you can control the humidity, you can inject a small amount of moisture into the meat while you are baking. It turns out that you get a succulent, marvelous roast because of that small amount of moisture allowed in the cavity.

Here is a quick recipe to try if you are lucky enough to have this oven. Take extra large baking potatoes. Using steam only, cook potatoes for 15 to 20 minutes, depending on size, then turn the steam off and bake until a toothpick slides easily in and out of the potato (around fifteen to twenty minutes). The flavor and texture will be better than potatoes that have been just steamed, baked, microwaved or boiled.

For that small kitchen where you have minimal room, one convection oven plus the Combo can replace a double oven and microwave. One important difference between this unit and the one previously described is the way it is installed. The combo oven is plumbed directly to a water source and drained as well— there is no reservoir for the cook to fill, nor any water to be removed when you are finished cooking. This offers greater convenience, but also makes the machine more expensive to purchase and install. Still and all, you get full value for the buck you are spending.

Oven Features

A few general notes on ovens: all ovens have thermostats. Manufacturers calibrate their ovens very carefully but over time or with frequent use the calibrations can be off. The best way to check your oven's true temperature, if you have any doubt, is to buy an oven gauge at a kitchen supply store. If there is a discrepancy and you've had the oven less than a year, most manufacturers will come out and fix it for free.

Additional features that separate the mediocre from the outstanding oven can be difficult to ascertain—one of the most important features of an oven, and one not always apparent to the consumer, is door insulation. How hot does the door get when the oven is on? Because showrooms usually have non-functioning appliances on display, that information can be difficult to track down. The best source is someone who has already purchased the appliance in question or a demonstration kitchen with working appliances. The oven door will be warm to the touch—that's normal—but you should have no problem leaving your hand on the door for an extended period of time. If the oven door is too hot to touch for more than a couple of seconds, then the oven door is not properly insulated. Manufacturers improve insulation with specialty door seals, multiple layers of glass, or air-flow vents that cool the door, just to name a few methods.

A few manufacturers produce ovens where the door opens to the side, like a fridge, rather than folding down to make a shelf. The first problems this poses is one of landing—where do you set the turkey while you baste it? Think how aggravating it would be to take something out of the oven, set it on an adjacent countertop (leaving the door open this whole time and losing all the heat in the oven) only to have to lift it back into the oven when you were finished testing it. The problem grows exponentially if the item is heavy or awkward. One way to solve this dilemma is to build a pull-out shelf into the oven cabinet; something similar to the pull-out cutting boards many kitchens have near the sink. This would give you a landing space where your oven door normally would be. But there are other factors to consider. First, a blast of hot air will hit you in the face if you are standing too close to the door when you open it. In addition, you must pay close attention to where you put your hands. It is easy for the back of your hand to accidently graze the open door as you slide something onto the racks. To its credit, this oven is a wonderful solution to the problem of access for the physically disadvantaged because a person in a wheelchair does not have to reach across a hot door to remove product.

• **Controls, Timers and Probes**. Control panels vary widely from oven to oven. Simpler, more economical ovens will have mechanical controls—a knob for temperature, a timer and that's about it. Convection ovens are often controlled by electronic keypads rather than knobs, which can be more complex to manipulate but also give the cook more choices, and often better results. Some of the best ovens on today's market has a sophisticated thermostat that keeps the temperature in the oven within one degree of where you set it.

Other features available in high-end ovens may be more labor-saving niceties than essential requirements. For example, some ovens will Look for oven racks that slide out more than half-way and remain, stable even with a heavy weight on them. give you a rotisserie attachment or a temperature probe that helps the home cook by telling him when a roast has reached the required temperature. Many of these ovens will also convert radiant oven recipes to convection times and temperatures automatically. As technology improves, many companies are coming out with tools to give the busy home cook control over her cooking without putting additional pressure on her schedule. One example is a recently released oven that is not only an oven, but a refrigerator as well. You can put your meal— be it a casserole, a whole chicken, or some other dish—into the oven (set in refrigerator mode) in the morning. Then just before leaving work at the end of the day, call or log on to the Internet to start the cooking. It even has a warming setting so that if you get stuck in traffic, your meal will be ready when you are.

• **Self-Cleaning**. Self-cleaning cycles are common on all but the most basic ovens. There are two methods manufacturers use. The first is pyrolytic self-cleaning, where the oven has a high temperature cycle distinct from other baking. During this cycle the oven heats up to 850 to 950 degrees. The oven door automatically locks during the high heat phase until temperatures are back within a safer range. The high heat phase lasts two to four hours and the cooling phase lasts an additional two hours, so the entire cleaning process can take as much as six hours to complete. Any grease or other residue in the oven gets turned into a fine ash that can be easily wiped clean with a sponge once the cycle is complete. Most manufacturers caution that the oven racks must be removed during this process so read your manual carefully before including any racks or other accessories.

In contrast to the high-temperature cycle, some ovens use a catalytic system, also known as the continuous cleaning method. In these models, the porcelain interior of the oven is designed to allow grease and oils to burn off during normal baking temperatures—the oven cleans itself with normal use. With that method, the oven racks and windows will require traditional cleaning. Starchy or sugary spills will create a crust on the floor of the oven that the catalytic system can't handle, so consider lining the bottom of the oven with foil. If such spills occur, simply replace the foil. Never use chemicals to clean a continuously cleaning oven—they will affect the porcelain enamel and make it unable to do its job.

• **Oven Racks**. One area of design where superior construction is most easily visible is the racks used to support the food. In economical and mid-range models, you will be lucky if the racks are able to come even halfway out of the oven—and when they do, they may wobble precariously. Better models will allow you to pull the rack almost all the way out and will remain stable even when fully extended. Some oven racks will even slide completely forward on ball-bearing rollers. That is obviously a desirable feature, but becomes more so if your ovens are below counter level. Bending down and reaching in, then supporting the food with one hand while you check it with the other is an experience we are all familiar with and would rather not re-create in a newly remodeled kitchen.

• **Warming Drawers**. The key to warming drawers is to carefully seal the food in plastic wrap or foil so that the moisture does not escape, thereby preserving the quality of what you've cooked. Be careful, do not allow food to stay too long, as you could have a prob-

Warning drawers are excellent for proofing dough and warming plates. If it's a question of budget, know that your oven can do the same.

lem with bacteria growth, in addition to destroying the taste and texture of the food. They are excellent for proofing dough and warming plates. If it's a question of budget, know that your oven can do the same.

There is one model designed to be used either with food

or in the bathroom as a towel warmer. All in all, they make a convenient addition to a kitchen appliance suite. However, they are somewhat pricey. If it comes down to dollars, prioritize a better oven or cooktop and forego the warming drawer in favor of the appliances you will use with greater frequency.

Warming drawers of yesteryear consisted of a twenty-five watt light bulb on an extension cord, placed in a thick glass or ceramic crock. The baker would set the dough on top of the crock and the steady heat from the bulb would create an even temperature for the dough, no matter what the time of year. When ovens had pilot lights, they also were used for proofing dough.

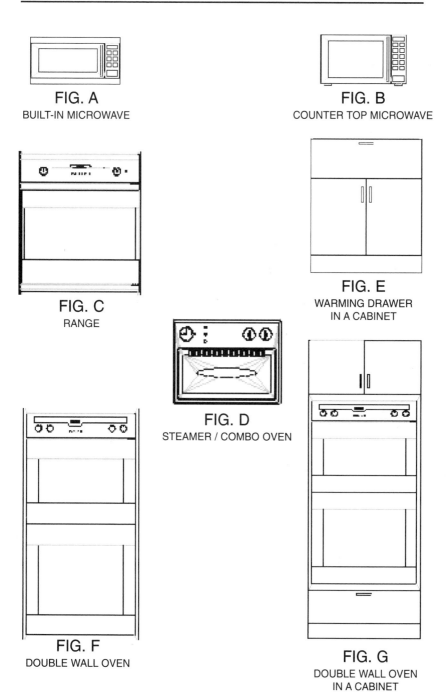

FIG. A
BUILT-IN MICROWAVE

FIG. B
COUNTER TOP MICROWAVE

FIG. C
RANGE

FIG. E
WARMING DRAWER
IN A CABINET

FIG. D
STEAMER / COMBO OVEN

FIG. F
DOUBLE WALL OVEN

FIG. G
DOUBLE WALL OVEN
IN A CABINET

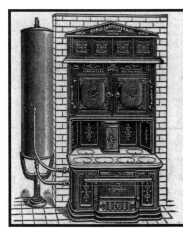

Ranges

A range is a cooktop and oven combined in the same unit, designed mainly for space savings, so the lessons from the cook-top and oven chapters apply here. The average range measures 30-inches wide, which accounts for the same problems cooktops suffer: the burners are too small and don't generate enough heat.

Types of Ranges

There are several types of ranges available. Starting with the most common, they are free-standing, slide-in and drop-in. Free-standing models sit directly on the floor. They can be placed between two cabinets or on their own (hence the name). These models have a raised area behind the burners that has a clock, timer and typically, oven and burner controls. Although inexpensive, these units suffer from the burner problems we mentioned above and have the added dysfunction of forcing you to reach over hot burners and pans to adjust the controls (See Illustration Figure A, Page 55). Slide-in ranges, as their name implies, are designed to fit neatly between two cabinets. They sit directly on the floor but the sides are unfinished. They have a lip in front and on top that fits over the cabinets and countertops to create a tight fit without the gaps that are common with free-standing ranges. These models usually do not have the raised area behind them; in the best versions, the knobs are in the front. Less well-designed units have the knobs on top, either in the middle of the burners where they get in the way, or to one side (See Illustration, Figure B, Page 55). Drop-in ranges are still a combined cooktop and oven, but instead of sitting on the floor they rest on a platform made of the same material as the cabinets.

Luckily for the home cook, an alternative type of range is on the market today, incorporating the multi-purpose cooktop we discussed in the cooktop chapter (See Illustration, Figures C and D, Page 55). This type of range looks commercial but is specifically made for the home. It is insulated so it can butt up against cabinets without scorching them, and the burners are sparked by electronic ignition. They come in sizes that vary from 30- to 60-inches wide, and 24- to 32-inches deep. The deeper ranges project beyond standard 24-inch base cabinets, so make sure that projection won't create traffic problems.

Gas, Electric, or Both?

Ranges can be gas powered, electric or have dual fuel. Dual fuel ranges have gas burners and electric, usually convection, ovens. The 48- and 60-inch models are available with two ovens. Some of these models have one convection, one radiant oven and some have two convection ovens. The convection option will add dollars, but in our experience, it's well worth it. Some high-end all-gas or dual-fuel ovens offer the option of hav-

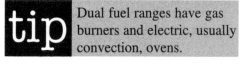

tip

Dual fuel ranges have gas burners and electric, usually convection, ovens.

ing a gas infrared broiler. This is by far the best broiler on the market. It has truly high, consistent heat and will broil faster and far more evenly than traditional gas or electric elements.

One range manufacturer offers a unique, well designed mixture of these features. It is a 48-inch range with two equally-sized ovens. One of the ovens is gas with an infrared broiler. The other is an electric convection oven. The combination of two large ovens is an excellent feature: many other manufacturers offer one extremely large oven and one much smaller oven— some are too small even for a slim cookie sheet. Since a large turkey will fit into both ovens of this unique range, it offers the cook far more flexibility. In the ranges with one big and one small oven, you would be stuck if you had to use the large oven for one large dish—the smaller (usually not convection) could handle at most two items. In this model, you could put your turkey or rib roast in the gas oven and put up to four different items on the racks of the convection oven. That's a lot more cooking power in the same amount of space. In addition to the well-designed ovens, this range also offers a convertible grill and griddle set (See pages 22 and 24 for a definition of these appliances). You can switch from gas grill to a griddle. Most other models require you to choose one or the other—or give up four burners to have both. This will do both in the space of two burners, though not at the same time.

Another range offers two same-size electric convection ovens and also includes two warming drawers beneath them. This is one of the few multi-purpose ranges sized to be inline with standard 24-inch deep counters. Although it means you will lose some burner space on top of the range, it may be worth it for kitchens with a crowded pathway. This model has six burners with the two high-powered central burners having 20,000 BTUs.

Be careful to compare all features and their frequency of use before you make a final decision. It doesn't make sense to give up better burners for the best broiler or oven or rack system in the world if you use the burners everyday and the oven twice a month. Speaking of racks, that is one area where there is a lot of difference from model to model. Like wall ovens, a clear sign of superior construction is racks that can be pulled out as far forward as possible. Some even slide forward on ball bearings.

A range's big plus is that it saves high frequency use counter space. While it may be more ergonomically sound to have your oven in a tall cabinet, you need to think carefully about how often you use your oven versus your counters.

Also, if you decide to invest in a range that has gas burners with high BTUs, be aware that it may require a three-quarter inch gas line instead of the standard half-inch. Be sure to check manufacturer's specifications, as they can change anytime.

tip Oven racks are a design feature where there is a lot of difference from model to model. A clear sign of superior construction is racks that can be pulled out as far forward as possible. Some even slide forward on ball bearings.

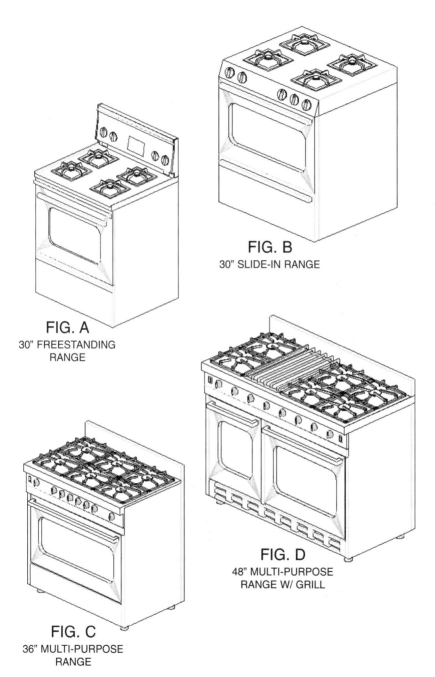

FIG. A
30" FREESTANDING
RANGE

FIG. B
30" SLIDE-IN RANGE

FIG. C
36" MULTI-PURPOSE
RANGE

FIG. D
48" MULTI-PURPOSE
RANGE W/ GRILL

All drawings copyright of 20/20 Software, version 6.1

A beautiful 1938 air-conditioned ice refrigerator like this only $67.50 f. o. b. factory ... Other models $49.50 to $94.50.

Refrigeration

Cold food storage is essentially no different than dry food storage. They are both pantries. Refrigerator manufacturers like you to think in terms of cubic feet. Resist! Think instead in terms of shelf space. By doing so, you'll be much better able to assess your needs and find the appliance that addresses those needs.

Size and Configuration

When you shop for a refrigerator, you will have a choice of side-by-side (refrigerator on right side, freezer on left), top freezer (freezer on top, refrigerator below), and bottom freezer (refrigerator on top, freezer below), in widths that include 24-, 27-, 30-, 33-, 36-, 42- and 48-inch (See Illustration, Page 71). Currently, only the side by side models are available in widths greater than thirty-six inches. Be aware that manufacturers written specifications often change. In addition, a unit may be called a 48-inch model and in reality be over or under that size. To protect yourself, always order your appliances ahead of time and have the contractor measure the actual machine before he builds the cabinet enclosure or places the electrical outlets.

Most people use a refrigerator far more than a freezer. The general rule is that a person goes to the refrigerator between 17 and 21 times more often than the freezer. The freezer-top model is therefore the least useful model, as you must bend continuously to retrieve anything. Even

 Most people use a refrigerator far more than a freezer. The general rule is that a person goes to the refrigerator between 17 and 21 times more often than the freezer.

though it is the most energy efficient model on the market (it may save you $20 a year on your electric bill), think about the human energy it wastes. However, don't even think of choosing between 36-inch side-by-side or a 36-inch freezer-top. The alleged convenience and larger capacity of a 36-inch side-by-side is wasted since the freezer takes up disproportionate space for its frequency of use. Vital refrigerator space has been sacrificed and the result is a refrigerator incapable of accommodating a number of bowls or platters of food prepared ahead of time for a party.

The narrow width of the refrigerator side of a 36-inch side-by-side combined with depth of up to 34-inches means you have volume without accessibility, which is like having a fast car with bad brakes—it doesn't do you much good. The best configuration for a 36-inch wide refrigerator/freezer combination is to have the freezer on the bottom as a pullout drawer.

If you are attracted by units with the icemaker in the door, currently you must choose between a side-by-side or top-freezer model. Bottom-freezer refrigerators are sometimes offered with chilled water in the door but no ice. Don't let that feature outweigh the practical usage of your refrigerator; if you must have a dispenser, invest in the 42- or 48-inch size. For the installation of such models make sure you have excess copper tubing for the water line so that when the refrigerator needs to be serviced, it can be pulled forward without disconnecting the line.

The only practical advantage of a 36-inch side-by-side refrigerator is the shallow door swing. In tight spaces like galley kitchens or between an island and a counter, the deep open door of a single-door refrigerator can be a traffic obstruction. Luckily, manufacturers are now making café-door refrigerators, also known as French door or armoire-style models. These units have a fridge top with freezer bottom configuration like many other units. The difference is the upper refrigerator portion has two doors that open in the center. You can open one or both doors and the interior remains undivided (See Illustration, Figure B, Page 71). They are best used in kitchens that have a counter or an island across from the refrigerator because when both doors are open, the counter space to the right and left sides is obstructed by the doors. Café-door refrigerators are generally 28- to 30-inches deep.

By the way, refrigerator depth statistics can be misleading. The depth measurement can refer to the case depth (without the door), the case depth plus door closed, or the case depth plus the door and handle. When we give measurements here, it will always be case depth without the door, as that is the most critical dimension when it comes to determining how a refrigerator will relate to the counters and cabinets around it.

Single-door refrigerators can be hinged to open either right or left, depending on your space. Refrigerator doors on side-by-sides, whether the 36-, 42-, or 48-inch model, usually hinge only on the right (See Illustration, Figures C and G, Page 70). Thus, in designing with a side-by-side in mind, both the sink and the countertop must be to the left or you will constantly have to walk around your refrigerator door to put anything down. Picture yourself reaching into such a refrigerator and pulling out a quart of milk in one hand and a plate of butter in the other. How do you shut the door? Your choices are to use your foot or your backside. This bears repeating: placing the sink and the countertop to the left of a side-by-side is essential.

Refrigerators and freezers are also available as completely separate units, rather than the combined units we have been discussing up to this point. These models are available as either freestanding or built-in units and range in size from 27- to 36-inches wide and up to 84-inches high (See Illustration, Figures D and E, Page 71). The size of these units requires a large kitchen or you risk losing function by losing counter space. One advantage is that they can be installed on opposite sides of the room to improve flow, if need be. Since you go to the refrigerator 21 times for every one time you go to the freezer, it can be advantageous to separate the units and place the refrigerator according to its high frequency use, with the freezer in another part of the kitchen.

Free Standing Refrigerators

In addition to the questions of size and configuration, you will need to decide if you want a freestanding, counter-depth, or built-in model. Freestanding refrigerators are the ones we all know well. They are usually 30- to 36-inches wide, 64- to 72-inches tall, and anywhere from 29- to 36-inches deep. This last figure—the depth—poses a few problems. On the practical side, a deep refrigerator makes it difficult to see everything, or even most, of what you have when you open the door. It takes work—shifting, peering, re-arranging—before you have a clear idea of what you are currently storing and what you need to purchase. That leads to several problems for the home cook—the famous "science experiment" syndrome being the most serious. Although this type of refrigerator is the least expensive to manufacture and purchase, it wastes money throughout the lifespan of the appliance. You can't see what you have, so you purchase duplicate items. You don't know what's there, so it rots before you can use it. Add to that the frustration you feel every time you go to clean it out or look for a specific item and the money you saved doesn't seem quite so important.

Sometimes, people are tempted to build-in a freestanding refrigerator to achieve a seamless look at a lesser cost. However, only refrigerators with forced air condensers (having a fan to circulate air) can be installed that way. A refrigerator with a standard static condenser will build up too much heat, resulting in potential damage to the compressor and much less efficient cooling.

Counter-Depth Refrigerators

The depth of freestanding refrigerators is also a problem of looks. At 29- to 36-inches deep, they can be up to a foot deeper than your 24-inch deep base cabinets. They stick out from your counters and look terrible—not like an integral part of your kitchen but like something that doesn't quite belong—not exactly the result you want after the months and money spent remodeling your kitchen. Enter the counter-depth freestanding refrigerator. As its name implies, this is a standard refrigerator that is shallower than other machines. The case of the refrigerator is 24-inches —just like your cabinets—with the door adding another two to three inches of depth. It looks much better than a standard freestanding model, and the reduced shelf depth certainly makes the storage space more accessible. There's just one problem. Counter-depth models are normal machines, usually the 36-inch size, that have been shrunk. The depth lost means the volume of storage is less than that of a freestanding model and certainly less than the average family of four needs if they shop for groceries once a week.

When Moorea first moved to France, she couldn't understand how the French could survive with their miniscule refrigerators (most of them were about as tall as a six-year old child and no deeper or wider than a dishwasher). What she discovered was that there was an enormous farmers market held every Tuesday, Thursday, and Saturday. A smaller market was held every day. Moorea's host mother would visit the market every two to three days. The vegetables she purchased never even made it into the refrigerator. That is a wonderful "Slow-Food" concept but let's face it—it's completely unrealistic given the pace at which we live our lives. So while the counter-depth refrigerator offers an alternative to the freestanding models, it doesn't really offer a solution.

Built-in Refrigerators

The built-in refrigerator differs in several key ways from freestanding and counter-depth models. First, we need to talk about what it means to be "built-in." These machines are 24 inches deep and do not have finished sides. They are designed to slide into a cabinet shell and blend in with the rest of your kitchen. All of them are available with paneled door fronts, meaning the front of your refrigerator matches your cabinets rather than being black, white, or stainless steel. Some models cannot be distinguished at all from the cabinetry around them.

Built-in units are available in 27-, 36-, 42-, and 48-inch widths. Most models are 84-inches high, with some models coming in at 73-inches. The compressor, or motor, of the appliance is usually above or below the storage area in a separate compartment. That means the full height, width, and depth of the storage area is available to be used without the usual nooks and crannies that show up in freestanding models. The height and the openness of the interior makes up for the lost depth. When combined with the larger widths, you get better storage accessibility and much greater volume. Imagine seeing everything that's there in a glance—you don't have to touch a thing.

Now imagine you're having a dinner party. You decide to make the salad ahead of time and dress it right before you serve it. You get out your largest bowl, put the salad together and go to put it in the fridge. Does it fit? The Tuscan pork loin you're serv-

tip Not every container you own will fit into a built-in refrigerator. You will most likely have to give up large square and round containers for rectangular ones. If you are really concerned, measure your favorite pieces and compare them with the interior dimensions of the models you are considering.

ing as an entrée is already there, stuffed with garlic, rosemary and olive oil, with a salt crust. You stuffed that last night to cut down on the things you need to do today. How much do you have to re-arrange, or even throw away, to be able to prepare for your party at a leisurely, relaxed pace so that when your guests arrive, there is a minimum to do and you can happily spend time with them? You begin to see that a too-small refrigerator can limit your menu and create stress—and not just when you entertain, but every time you have to spend five minutes trying to find the mayonnaise or decide whether it's worse to open the plastic container or just throw it away.

Not every container you own will fit into a built-in refrig-erator. You will most likely have to give up large square and round containers for rectangular ones. If you are really concerned, measure your favorite pieces and compare them with the interior dimensions of the models you are considering. While freestanding refrigerators may have one to two shelves a few inches deeper that those of a built-in, not all of the shelves will be deeper and some of them will be shallower. That is due to the mechanics of freestanding machines being hidden within the storage area itself. The top two shelves of a freestanding machine are usually the deepest; as you work your way down to the bottom, the shelves and drawers get smaller and smaller. What looks like lots of space at eye level disappears very quickly. That is not true of built-in refrigerators. The separate component area above or below means you have full use of your shelves, side to side and front to back. That is why it is so crucial to look at shelf space and ignore cubic footage.

We noted earlier that a 36-inch side-by-side freestanding refrigerator is the worst machine you can have. Well, the built-in version is no better. In fact, it may be worse because the narrow width of each area is rendered more useless by also being shallow. You may not lose any foodstuffs to decay, but mostly because there is no room to put anything in there to begin with. That leaves us with 42- and 48-inch side-by-side models. Let's look at the 48-inch model. That's right—a four foot refrigerator. The interior dimensions are what really count. The refrigerator side of these models is usually within an inch above or below 25-inches wide. The freezer side hovers around 15-inches in most manufacturers. What's interesting about this fact is that when you move to the 42-inch models, you go from 25-inches in the refrigerator side to around 20-inches—that's a twenty percent loss. Your freezer side narrows by an inch to two inches—around a ten percent loss. When you drop down to the 36-inch side-by-sides, you lose thirty percent of your refrigerator space, as compared to the 48-inch, and around ten to twenty percent in the freezer. These may seem like small numbers until you are preparing for a dinner party or a holiday meal or just trying to put away groceries. Five inches can mean the difference between success and delight or disaster and frustration.

In addition to the size benefits and the integrated style of built-in refrigerators, some models are even better at keeping food fresh. Consistent interior temperature and humidity is the way this is accomplished. Almost all built-ins have better insulation than their freestanding counterparts but more importantly, their cooling technology is more sophisticated. One company uses two compressors—one for the freezer and one for the fridge. That means that your freezer temperature doesn't drop every time you open the fridge door, which translates into a lot less freezer burn, decay, and other problems you face with a freestanding model. Another company accomplishes the same thing with a single compressor and a sensitive thermostat that keeps the compartment within one degree of where you set it. The method the company uses to achieve temperature consistency is not important—just that they do it. As you can imagine from the list of benefits of built-in refrigerators, they are more expensive than freestanding models. Let us pose the question, how much are you willing to pay for convenience, efficiency, and ease? As we stated in the introduction, the appliances you put in your kitchen will determine your ease and delight when working in your kitchen. **Prioritize your dollars and put your money where you will have tangible use of it—in the appliances.**

Undercounter Refrigeration

Refrigeration options multiply when you consider that there are now under-counter refrigerator units and freezer units that can be installed anywhere they add to convenience. Most are 24- or 27-inches deep and are available with drawer or door-style access (See Illustration, Figures A and H, Page 71). The small size of these units allows them to fit into unusual or simply small spaces. Imagine the flexibility of storing produce at the prep island, drinks and snacks in the family room and frozen meats in the pantry. These machines work beautifully as additions to standard refrigerators. The choices are endless and this type of flexibility is important in large kitchens where point-of-use storage is critical in streamlining the cooking process.

Commercial-Look Refrigeration

Some people like the look of commercial refrigerators. Truly commercial refrigeration is too large to fit nicely into most kitchens. In addition, those models may not meet the energy-efficiency guidelines for home use of the EPA in your state. There are many models that have a commercial look to them. They come in a variety of sizes. They are all in stainless steel, some with stainless steel doors and others with glass doors. Glass doors, while attractive, don't offer many benefits. For instance, you can't have shelves on the door, and not everyone wants to display the contents of their refrigerator. However, glass door refrigeration will have deeper shelves.

Shelving And Food Storage

Shelf construction in refrigerators is usually either rod and frame or tempered glass. The tempered glass is far superior because it gives you greater visibility and makes clean up easier—spills are contained, rather than dripping from shelf to shelf. Separate compartments for meat and vegetables will allow you to create climate zones appropriate for what you are storing. For example, meat keeps better a few degrees colder than the rest of your refrigerator and many vegetables will do better in a sealed compartment that maintains a higher moisture level. A quick word of advice: don't overcrowd the drawers. Air needs to be able to circulate around items in order to cool them. All foods—but vegetables without skins especially (e.g. lettuce)—will last longer if stored in plastic bags or with some other air-tight covering so that they retain their moisture. Dehydration can happen overnight. In addition, strong food odors won't move into your ice bin or overcome the taste of delicate foods.

Most refrigeration manufacturers achieve zone temperatures and humidity control through drawers and other closures for butter, cold cuts, vegetables, and fruits. If you have to refrigerate them, tomatoes will survive best in the butter area, where the temperature is around 50 to 60 degrees. Be aware that though the tomatoes may last longer, refrigeration is quick to harm the fresh flavor of the fruit. Fish and shellfish will do best in the back of the refrigerator where the temperature is a few degrees colder because it is less affected by the opening and closing of the door. If you have any concerns about your refrigerator's temperature setting, buy two or three temperature gauges so you can test its different dial settings in different locations.

A final note on refrigeration: ideal internal temperature should range between 36 and 40 degrees Fahrenheit. By the way, this temperature is far too cold for storing white wine. White wine should be chilled to around fifty degrees. Any colder and the flavor is greatly diminished. If you want to keep white wines at pleasurable drinking temperatures, invest in a specially-made electric wine cellar. They are about two feet wide, two feet deep and 32-to 72-inches high (depending on the number of bottles you need to hold). Many inexpensive models will work well to keep your wine cold but if you want to build the machine into a cabinet, you will have to upgrade to a high-

 Built-in refrigerators—as they are more complex-machines require more maintenance than freestanding units. The area where the compressor is located—above or below the storage area—should be vacuumed once a month.

end model. If you are planning to store red wine for a year or more, then the cellar doesn't need to be kept so cool. Fifty-five degrees is an appropriate temperature for long-term preservation. The most important factor, however, is consistency of temperature. Swings of even a few degrees can adversely affect the quality of your wine when it comes time to drink it.

Wines should be stored between 43 and 53 degrees—the white wines closer to forty-three, the reds closer to fifty three. Serving wine is a whole different story. The whites and light reds range from 50 to 60 degrees, the big reds between 62 and 67 degrees.

Refrigerator Maintenance

The interior of refrigerators should be routinely washed and cleaned out. Spills should be wiped up immediately with warm soapy water as needed. It's a good idea to make cleaning out the interior of your fridge an item on your monthly to-do list.

You should check food items for decay at least weekly because spoiled vegetables release ethylene gas that will increase the speed of spoilage in fresh produce.

Built-in refrigerators are more complex machines and require more maintenance than freestanding units. The area where the compressor is located—above or below the storage area—should be vacuumed once a month. Like a car, these machines will need a tune-up once a year by a certified professional to stay in good working condition. Almost all the stories we've been told about poor quality built-ins were really about uneducated consumers not taking proper care of their investment. Don's built-in refrigerator is over fifteen years old, and in great shape.

Energy Efficiency

If you want to maximize the energy efficiency of your appliances, look for models that belong to the Energy Star program. These are units that are 15% more efficient than government regulations require. Many refrigerators are available that can reduce your energy consumption by up to 40% compared with a standard refrigerator just five years old. To find an

tip You should check food items for decay at least weekly because spoiled vegetables release ethylene gas that will increase the speed of spoilage in fresh produce.

energy efficient model with the features you want, go to the website energystar.gov.

To help conserve energy with your existing refrigerator, here are some things you can do: make sure the door seals are airtight. Keep the coils clean and allow air to flow around them.

Don't put your refrigerator near a heat source, like your oven or a sunny window. These and many more suggestions are available on the energystar.gov website.

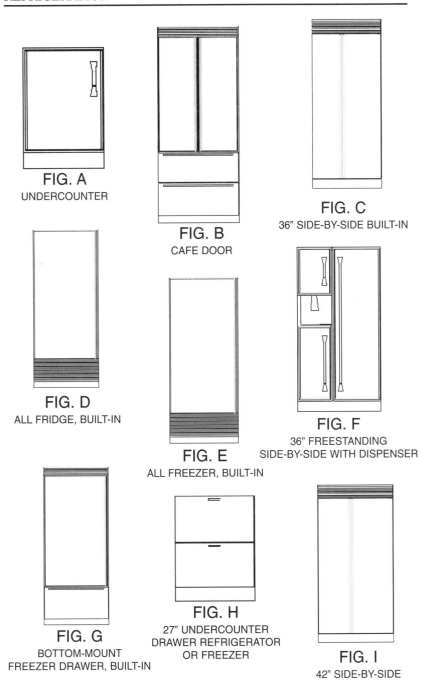

FIG. A
UNDERCOUNTER

FIG. B
CAFE DOOR

FIG. C
36" SIDE-BY-SIDE BUILT-IN

FIG. D
ALL FRIDGE, BUILT-IN

FIG. E
ALL FREEZER, BUILT-IN

FIG. F
36" FREESTANDING
SIDE-BY-SIDE WITH DISPENSER

FIG. G
BOTTOM-MOUNT
FREEZER DRAWER, BUILT-IN

FIG. H
27" UNDERCOUNTER
DRAWER REFRIGERATOR
OR FREEZER

FIG. I
42" SIDE-BY-SIDE

What Useless Drudgery!

Washing dishes by hand

FOR less than one cent's worth of electricity a day a Walker Electric Dishwasher washes your finest china cleaner, more safely, than you can do it by hand. Your hands keep lovely. You have time to spend precious hours with your family.

The new Walker Electric Dishwasher is proving a sensation in every part of the country. It eliminates 90% of the work with pots and pans, too.

Has only one moving part. It is built for a lifetime. There are built-in sink models in various sizes—also a portable cabinet model.

We invite you to try one in your own home. If it doesn't prove the greatest electric time and labor saver you have ever had, don't keep it. Mail the coupon.

WALKER
ELECTRIC DISHWASHERS
Sink and Cabinet Models

AC-11

Walker Dishwasher Corp.,
1024 S. Waller Ave., Chicago, Ill.

Send literature on the Walker Electric Dishwasher and names of nearby dealers.

Name ....

Address ....

....

Dishwashers

Lets talk for a moment about what a dishwasher is supposed to be. It is a labor saving device designed to sanitize dishes, serving ware, and silverware. The result should be dishes that are sparkling clean and bacteria-free. Most modern dishwashers will do that job well. What sets them apart are factors like capacity, ease of loading, water consumption and quietness.

Water Temperture And Cycle Times

Premium dishwashers have the ability to heat water to the proper temperature for sanitation and dissolving detergent, regardless of the incoming water temperature. Inexpensive models heat water on a timer, not a thermostat, therefore they are relying on the water heater to be at the correct temperature and not too far away from the kitchen. Premium models also have in-line heaters instead of heating coils in the bottom pan, thus eliminating plastic-ware meltdown.

It is a mystery to us why domestic dishwasher manufacturers do not produce residential dishwashers that process faster than the usual 60 to 120 minutes. If you're using the pots and pans cycle, it can take as long as 140 minutes. That's right,

tip Premium dishwashers have the ability to heat water to the proper temperature for sanitation and dissolving detergent, regardless of the incoming water temperature.

more than two hours. There are, admittedly, several commercial under-the-counter dishwashers that will do the job in four minutes, but these require 240 volts versus the usual 120. They do not dry dishes, and they are unkind to good china.

We know of one residential dishwasher on the market that offers a short, 35 minute cycle. What a great feature, especially for those times when you end an evening gathering and have multiple loads to do before bed. This machine has a sophisticated electronic brain that "reads" the soil level of the dishes and adjusts water pressure to compensate. While the short, high-pressure cycle isn't recommended for fine china, the machine does offer a special setting designed for washing these items.

Water Consumption

Many American made residential machines are water guzzlers, consuming 12 to 14 gallons per load, although that is beginning to change. European dishwashers, on the other hand, are leagues ahead in water consumption. A few have fast cycles that will do a good job, as long you do not include pots and pans in the load. For models that do not have a heated drying feature, look for units that have a vent in the door that allows the moist air to escape during the drying process. Models that use convection dry without this vent will not dry as well. Regarding water use, the frugal European machines use a mere four to five and a half gallons. Most are also quieter.

To Pre-Rinse Or Not

Most dishwashers today will wash dishes without pre-rinsing. Food particles either collect in a trap which is easily removed for cleaning, or are ground up in an internal disposal system and swept away. As a matter of fact, it is better for your dishes if you don't pre-rinse because dishwasher soap is highly alkaline. Without food residue to act on, the soap works directly on the dish surface, potentially etching it. The soap can also etch glasses and pit silverware. One of the ways you can combat this dishwasher wear and tear is to only fill the main soap compartment of the standard two. As it turns out, the water in the first rinse cycle usually isn't hot enough to dissolve the soap anyway.

Quality, Capacity, And Ease Of Loading

The better dishwashers have stainless steel interiors, with less expensive models using molded plastic. A rinse aid is necessary for the drying process in models with stainless steel interiors and will reduce spotting in all dishwashers.

Almost all dishwashers are a standard 24-inches wide (there are a few exceptions, like the 18-inch space saver models), so your choice of machine will not affect your space planning. If your kitchen is very large, or if you throw a lot of dinner parties or have big crowds, you may also want to put in a second dishwasher in the prep area. All dishwashers come 34- to 34 1/2-inches high, so fitting them under the standard 36-inch counter is no problem. However, if you wish to lower the counter, some European models come with adjustable legs that allow the dishwasher to be raised or lowered slightly.

Since the size of most dishwashers doesn't vary, it may seem confusing to you that we list capacity as one of our main criteria for judging the quality of a particular unit. There is a huge difference between different models and, as can be expected, the capacity and the price tag are directly connected. One of the best brands on the market has moved the booster (the additional water heater) from the bottom of the dishwasher to the side, allowing greater capacity. That unit also has a top rack designed just for silverware. It can hold much more than a standard dishwasher with just two racks and a silverware basket. And its more efficient: gone are the days of rewashing silverware.

Some manufacturers offer dishwasher drawers. These models have an edge over their door-style counterparts in ease-of-loading, but you give up a fair amount of capacity in trade. There are double-drawer models, taking up the same size as a standard dishwasher, or a single drawer, which takes up less space. The single drawer units can make a great second dishwasher in an island or butler's pantry. The second dishwasher, often full-size, is becoming very popular for families with large households or those who entertain frequently. We've all hosted a birthday dinner, or some other large get-together, where the dishwasher is full, running, and a sea of dishes remains piled on the counter. One caution about second dishwashers is that they need to be used at least once or twice a week or the seals will dry-out, crack, and the machine will no longer function properly. If you do decide to get one, make sure to alternate its use with your everyday dishwasher to keep them both in top condition.

The price difference in dishwashers is related to options. The least expensive come with one wash arm, stationary racks, and a choice of two cycles. Those in the medium price range offer two wash arms, two to four cycles, a filtering system, a sanitizing cycle that reaches upwards of 140 degrees and some insulation. The most expensive give you three wash arms, adjustable rack positions, adjustable length cycles, a separate silverware tray, a built-in air gap, and a hot water booster that raises the temperature by means of a sensor to upwards of 140 degrees and, in general, has far better insulation. Some even feature a built-in water softener, and most are ultra-quiet.

Another factor to consider is how you want the dishwasher to look. Many manufacturers are offering models that have panel-ready doors—meaning you can match the front of your dishwasher to your cabinets so that it blends in seamlessly with its surroundings (See Illustration, Figure C, Page 79).

The support racks are one of the most important features of your dishwasher. Even though they may seem unimportant compared to looks, the right racks can make loading the dishwasher faster and easier. Since that is a chore some families have to do multiple times a day, it is worth investing in the right kind of racks. Flexibility is a key factor. Inexpensive machines give you no options—the racks are immovable. Step up a level in quality and you will have the ability to remove or relocate the prongs that hold the plates upright, so that you can accommodate large bowls. The very best machines allow you to customize every part of every shelf to suit the items you are using—be they glasses, small or large plates or even very large serving dishes. Several manufacturers allow the top rack to be adjusted at an angle, so that extra large plates can fit under it on one side and tall wine glasses rest on top of the rack on other side.

Food Safety

Although we don't always talk about food safety, the most important function of your dishwasher is preserving the health of you and your family. Most cooks are aware of the dangers of cross-contamination. For example, knives used to cut up raw chicken need to be sanitized before they can be used to cut up vegetables that will be eaten raw. But we often ignore simple dishwasher maintenance that can prevent the wash water from reaching the right sanitizing temperatures. Clogged wash arms and poor water pressure are risk factors that can significantly undermine your dishwasher's ability to do its job.

Energy Efficiency

If you want to maximize the energy efficiency of your appliances, look for models that belong the Energy Star program. These are units that are 25% more efficient than government regulations require. Many dishwashers are available that can reduce your energy costs by more than $25 a year. More importantly, they reduce pollution. To find an energy efficient model with the features you want, go to the website energystar.gov.

Whether you have a typical dishwasher or an Energy Star model, you can be more energy efficient by waiting until you have a full load to run your dishwasher. Dry-heat cycles also use a lot of energy, so it is a good idea to use the air-dry option instead. Be aware that this will take a little longer to dry the dishes.

FIG. A
SINGLE DISHDRAWER
WITH CABINET

FIG. B
DOUBLE DISHDRAWER

FIG. C
DISHWASHER W/ FULL OVERLAY CABINET PANEL

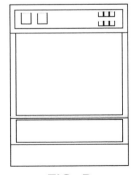

FIG. D
STANDARD DISHWASHER

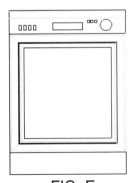

FIG. E
DISHWASHER W/ PARTIAL
OVERLAY CABINET PANEL

All drawings copyright of 20/20 Software, version 6.1

NOTES

Trash Compactors

Whenever a client requests a trash compactor, we wince. Knowing the many problems that can develop with them, our advice is to consider all the factors carefully. For starters, they create odors and attract insects and sometimes rodents, even when they are kept meticulously clean.

Although compactors come as large as 18-inches or as small as 12-inches wide, the interior capacity for trash in all units is quite small, as the compactor mechanism takes up as much as forty percent of the volume of the unit. While on the surface it seems that reducing the volume of your trash means making less trips to the trash can or dumpster, ask yourself, do you really want to leave trash in your house longer? In addition to problems of odor and animal attraction, compacted trash is four times as heavy as a comparable volume of un-compacted trash. You may find yourself having to empty the unit before you have even filled it so you can comfortably and safely carry it outside.

The idea behind trash compactors is well meaning. Squashing the trash to one-quarter its size saves precious landfill space. However, the compacted trash takes longer to break down in the ground, nullifying any potential benefit of its smaller size. In addition, many cities now require that citizens recycle separate types of trash, so having two distinct compartments is often far more useful. We prefer, instead, a recycling center located behind a door in a base cabinet next to the clean-up sink. That kind of recycling center is essentially a drawer which pulls out almost completely on gliders and has two attached wastebaskets—one for bottles and cans, the other for paper and packaging trash. This system allows for fast and easy separation, takes up less space and is far less expensive than a compactor.

One last caution–there are some compactors where the door remains locked if the machine breaks down, and the trash is trapped inside until a service professional fixes the machine. Better hope this doesn't happen to you on a three-day weekend.

If you decide that a compactor is the right waste solution for your kitchen, here are some things to look for: compacting pressure, ease of clean-up, quiet operation, and safety. Two thousand pounds of pressure is a minimum; some models have up to three thousand pounds. The interior should not have many nooks or crannies that are difficult to wipe clean. Unless you will be washing out all bottles and cans and other containers before you put them in the trash, expect spills and leaks on a regular basis. The bags can tear during the compaction process, so you want to make sure when that happens you can easily and quickly clean the interior. The motor of these machines is usually no louder than that of the garbage disposal, but additional sounds of metal crunching or glass breaking will create more noise. We don't recommend putting glass into compactors because the shards easily tear trash bags and make disposal more difficult and dangerous. All compactors have key locks and interruption switches that prevent the unit from compacting when the drawer is open. These features will typically ensure safety.

Be judicious with the items you put in your compactor. Any toxins, chemical compounds that could adhere to the unit, or combustible items should never be put into a compactor.

NOTES

Hoods/Ventilation Systems

Despite the critical role ventilation plays in removing pollutants like smoke, moisture, and gasses, the kitchen's ventilation system is often an afterthought for many clients. In fact, ventilation is critical to the proper and healthy functioning of any kitchen. Ventilation systems should be considered as important a purchase as any other major appliance.

Types of Ventilation Systems

There are a variety of ventilating systems on the market today, including ceiling and wall fans (which are basically worthless), re-circulating units (which merely move air around in the hood and back into the room) and downdraft and updraft extraction systems (which move air to the outside of the home). Re-circulating units don't work at all. They have charcoal filters that are supposed to remove pollutants from the air before returning it to the room, but they are so inefficient that they are worthless. In addition, the charcoal filters are expensive and need to be replaced frequently. Downdraft units have to work against the laws of physics, because the hot, dirty air coming off your cooktop wants to rise and expand and the downdraft is trying to pull it in the opposite direction from where it wants to go. The only ventilation system that really works well is an updraft unit. Updraft units consist of several parts: a hood, filter, lights and switches, motors, and ducting from the hood in the kitchen to the outside of the house. The blower (or motor) pulls smoke through the filter, then out through a duct cut into the roof or the side of the house.

What Makes A Hood Work?

The efficiency of hood and ventilation systems is rated in cubic feet per minute of air movement, or CFMs. Since vapors rise, you want to make sure you have a large enough container, or plenum, to catch all that pollution. Rather than delve into the technical aspects, let me simply describe what you need.

The hood should extend 3-inches beyond each side of your cooktop or range, 6-inches on each side if you also have a charbroiler. For example, if your cooktop or range is 36-inches wide, your hood should be 42-inches wide. When there is no charbroiler, the depth of the hood should be at least the depth of your range or cooktop. we prefer 3-inch beyond manufacturers recommendations. You'll never miss the six inches of cabinet space like you would miss a clean, well-ventilated kitchen.

Adequate ventilation design requires a balanced treatment of air removal, capture, and interior heating or air conditioning. The capture area of a hood is critical and often overlooked. It refers to a cavity designed to collect dirty air before it spreads into the room. For example, most hood manufacturers require their hood be placed 30-inches higher than the cooktop. In most kitchens, this puts the bottom of the hood at 5-feet 6-inches from the floor of the kitchen—not the best location for the average adult. The reason for this specification is that hood manufacturers know that 9 times out of 10 a client with a 30-inch range will buy a 30-inch hood. But pollutants don't rise in a straight line—they expand as they move towards the ceiling. Adequate capture area requires that the hood be wide enough (at least 3-inches wider than the cooktop on each side) and deep enough to collect this dirty air so that the motor can then remove it. Any air that isn't captured first will not be removed from the kitchen. At some point or another, you have probably forgotten to turn on the hood and ended up with a room full of odors or smoke. Have you noticed that turning on the hood at that point doesn't do any good? A motor powerful enough to pull smoke from outside of a hood canopy would also be powerful enough pull your food right off the cooktop, not to mention being very noisy. This notion of capture area is too often ignored, not only in hood specification, but also in hood design. There are many sleek, designer hoods on the marketplace today that are perfectly flat on the bottom—the filters are on the bottom of the hood with no cavity (known as a plenum) there to create a space to collect the polluted air. These models typically have around 300 CFMs. But in this hood design, CFMs don't matter. Even if they had 1000 CFMs, they couldn't adequately vent anything but the most impotent cooktop.

Height Of A Range Hood

Lets go back to the question of the hood's height from the floor for a moment. Despite the guidelines of some manufacturers, the height of the bottom of the hood is most appropriately determined by the height of the tallest cook—the increased height will not affect the efficiency of the hood, as long as it has sufficient CFMs to draw out all the waste and is at least six inches wider than the cooktop. Many times I have put the bottom of the hood 72- to 76-inches off the finished floor rather than the standard 57- to 66-inches, so that taller people can walk under the hood without banging their heads against it.

Selecting Hood Blowers

You have choices in the placement of your hood blowers: in-hood or remote (which can be either in-line or external). In-hood motors are exactly what they sound like, located within the vent-hood itself. They offer the simplest installation. However, the size of the hood will limit the size of the motors and therefore the number of CFM (cubic feet per minute) the motor will be able to move. The size of the duct is determined by the amount of CFMs. Be sure to check with manufacturers' specifications as to what size duct is needed. For example, generally the multi-purpose six-burner cooktops will require a 10" duct. The next option, in-line blowers, separates the hood from the motor. Your hood would

tip The height of the bottom of the hood is most appropriately determined by the height of the tallest cook—the increased height will not affect the efficiency of the hood, as long as it has sufficient CFMs to draw out all the waste and is at least six inches wider than the cooktop.

contain lights, switches and filters, but the motor is located at a midpoint in the duct (usually in an attic) between the hood and the exit port on the roof or wall. The last variety is an external blower, consisting of a motor mounted on the roof or on the side of the house within a protective housing. Obviously, the model you choose will depend in part on the details of your installation—for example, you would not want to put an externally-mounted motor on the roof where it could be seen from the street. Both inline and external-mount motors have a few advantages over in-hood motors. First, the size of the motors is not restricted by the size of the hood. The remote location also reduces the noise you hear in the kitchen. You will still hear the movement of air through filters, but there will be little or no sound from the motor itself.

We've often had people ask why the hood doesn't pull the smoke out completely. We've suggested opening a window and, lo and behold, it works. In commercial kitchen design, we worry about pulling out pollutants and replacing them with clean air (i.e., make up air). In a residential kitchen, opening a window will usually do the trick. If you live in a location with severe winters, you will need to consider incorporating a system for make-up air into your home's heating, ventilation and air-conditioning (HVAC) plan. We believe that you should have some form of fire retardant system. Consult a local company specializing in fire-control systems for information on what would be appropriate for your kitchen.

On occasion, we've had to use downdraft ventilation systems which pull the smoke down and out a floor duct under the house. That is necessary when the cooktop is on an island and you don't want to use a hood because it appears too massive or you can't vent up structurally. In those situations, cooktops generally require one of two kinds of ventilation systems—one lies flat, centered between the burners; the other rises 7- to 12-inch behind the cooktop. Of the two, there is no question that the latter is superior. It is elevated over the cooktop, giving it a better chance to catch pollutants. However, both are imperfect because they cannot capture all the rising vapors the way a plenum can.

In addition to those concerns, ventilation is further complicated behind the scenes by the path the air has to move through from the kitchen to the exterior of the house. To be precise, the shorter and straighter the duct, the better your ventilation will work. If you have any concerns about your ventilation, consult an expert. Sometimes your local appliance dealer will have all the information you need. However, not all dealers or salespeople are knowledgeable about ventilation; if you have any misgivings, hire a design professional with experience specifying the kind of appliances you want.

Products We'd Like to See Manufactured

A wall cabinet with a compressor, so we can store oils at 50 degrees to keep them from turning rancid.
A salamander or cheese-melter for home use.
A wall oven with a gas infrared broiler.
An undercounter wine cooler with completely separate, divided drawers for whites and reds.
An undercounter blast freezer around 18- to 24-inches wide.
A 12- to 18-inch drop-in gas charbroiler.

We would like to see the tail stop wagging the dog. Appliance manufacturers should set standard sizes and specs, not the cabinet companies! Cabinets can be cut any number of ways, but you can't cut an appliance.

Books Available from NMI Publishers
18653 Ventura Blvd., Suite 547
Tarzana, CA 91356
To Order:
KITCHEN DESIGN WITH COOKING IN MIND
REVISED 2003 $29.95 **To Order: 800.900.4761**
By Donald E. Silvers
The title speaks for itself.

HOW TO RAISE MOSTLY HEALTHY CHILDREN
By Jerry Newmark $11.95 **To Order: 818.708.1244**
18345 Ventura Blvd., Suite 314, Tarzana, CA 91356
The title speaks for itself.

HAPPINESS THROUGH SUPERFICIALITY
The War Against Meaningful Relationships
by Jerry Newmark and Irving S. Newmark
(176 pages, 1992...$11.95)

This book lifts your spirits, make you laugh, challenges you to rethink your values and shows you how to lead happier, more fulfilling life. The Doctors Newmark offer fresh perspectives, in a humorous and often provocative way, on many of the most serious aspects of life-sex, marriage, parenting, work, health, education, money, love, lawyers, doctors, psychotherapy and much more. You will learn how to stop taking everything too seriously-especially your self and how to come through the '90s whole and happy.

THIS SCHOOL BELONGS TO YOU & ME:
Every Learner A Teacher, Every Teacher a Learner
by Gerald Newmark
(431 pages, 1976...$9.95)

First published in 1976, this book remains an important resource for anyone interested in improving education. It describes a new kind of learning community-an exciting school where students, parents, teachers, staff and administrators are turned on to learning and to working cooperatively with each other.

"This School Belongs To You & Me" offers a detailed plan for the redesign of an entire school in a vibrant learning community. It is also a rich resource book of educational ideas and practices which can be used by individual teachers to improve and existing program or classroom. Developed from a seven-year, Ford Foundation supported project in inner-city elementary schools, the ideas presented can be applied to all school levels, whatever their geographic, ethnic, or soci-economic characteristics, in exciting, cost-effective ways.

To order any of the above books, except KPWCIM send a check for the amount indicated, plus $3.00 for p&h (add$1 for each additional book) to: **NMI PUBLISHERS**, 18345 Ventura Blvd., Suite 314, Tarzana, CA 91356. For Credit Card orders call: 818-708-1244

Notes